Christmas 1987

To Alex,
Cause we wanted to know,
lend get ready for the next
one.
Love,
Mona

EX LIBRIS
PEGASUS

BLITZ

AN AUTOBIOGRAPHY

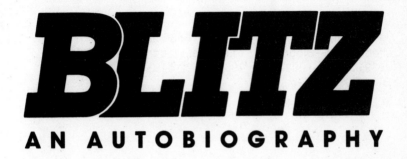

BLITZ

AN AUTOBIOGRAPHY

TOM JACKSON

WITH WOODROW PAIGE

CONTEMPORARY
BOOKS, INC.
CHICAGO ■ NEW YORK

Library of Congress Cataloging-in-Publication Data

Jackson, Tom, 1957–
  Blitz, an autobiography.

  Includes index.
  1. Jackson, Tom, 1957–   . 2. Football players—
United States—Biography. I. Paige, Woodrow. II. Title.
GV939.J33A3   1987   796.332′092′4 [B]   87-15695
ISBN 0-8092-4662-7

Copyright © 1987 by Tom Jackson and Woodrow Paige
All rights reserved
Published by Contemporary Books, Inc.
180 North Michigan Avenue, Chicago, Illinois 60601
Manufactured in the United States of America
Library of Congress Catalog Card Number: 87-15695
International Standard Book Number: 0-8092-4662-7

Published simultaneously in Canada by Beaverbooks, Ltd.
195 Allstate Parkway, Valleywood Business Park
Markham, Ontario L3R 4T8 Canada

For Katie Lane Jackson, who passed her spirit and sensitivity on to me. She hung out in the backyard so many afternoons throwing the football around with me. She never saw me play, but she must have known.

T.J.

And for my mom, Billie Paige, who was there at the beginning and will be with me until the end.

W.P.

CONTENTS

FOREWORD

EX LIBRIS
PEGASUS

When I was the running back coach with the Dallas Cowboys, one of my responsibilities was to look at films of the other teams' linebackers. We were getting ready to play Denver in the last regular-season game of 1977, and I saw this linebacker, Tom Jackson, for the first time. Since we were in the NFC and Denver was in the AFC, and we never played each other, I hadn't paid much attention to them. Well, I saw Tom flying all over the field and making tackles, and he intercepted a pass against Baltimore and ran it back for a touchdown. I was really impressed with him. In fact, I thought he was their best linebacker.

I've never told this before, but when we got ready to play Denver in the Super Bowl, we came up with this elaborate plan to neutralize Tom. He was their key player, and we couldn't leave him open on the weak side. So what we put in for the Super Bowl was a two-tight-end formation. Then, right before the game, we found

9

out Jay Saldi couldn't play, so we had to put in Butch Johnson, a wide receiver, instead, and we were frightened of what Jackson would do to us. That's the kind of effect he can have. You don't think a 215-pound linebacker can make a team change its offensive game plan, but that's Tom Jackson.

When I came to Denver as coach, my son was 13, and the first thing he said to me was he wanted to meet Tom Jackson. My own son's favorite player was Tom Jackson. *Everyone* loves Tom. If you don't like Tom, you don't like anybody.

Then we started practicing, and in all my time around football I've never seen anybody enjoy practice like Tom Jackson. Most everyone I ever was around hated to practice. But not Tom. He actually had fun. I never saw him have a bad practice or get mad at practice. That attitude was contagious. I think everyone else started having fun, too.

Every year we have a vote for the Most Inspirational Player, and I count the votes. I can tell every year right away that he's going to win. It's not even close. And if the coaches voted, Tom Jackson would get the award, too, because he inspires us.

The game should be played for fun, no matter how much money you make. And I think Tom is almost childlike in his enjoyment. He approaches it like a kid. He would have been just as happy playing in the 1940s for peanuts. More than anybody else on the team, he loves the game.

There was no doubt before the 1986 season that he was going to have a tough time making our team. He was coming off an injury, and it just didn't look like he could make it again. But nobody has ever worked any harder than Tom to come back.

Two or three years ago when we played the Raiders, Tom knocked a ball loose, and we recovered in the end zone for a touchdown. He was making plays all over the field. Whenever we played the Raiders, Tom was in the twilight zone for a whole week. Not that he does anything stupid or crazy; he just gears himself up even more when we play the Raiders. If we played the Raiders every week, he would never retire. He'd play against the Raiders until he died.

Tom never held anything back, so he was really the liaison between me and the players. If we were playing poorly, he was the guy I'd go to and talk to about our preparation, because I knew he'd get the word to the other players. After the Seattle game, at the end of last season, when we were embarrassed, I met with Tom to bounce some things off him, and he and I were thinking along the same lines. He thought we had to get our intensity back, so we returned to harder workouts, almost like training camp, and you could tell the difference.

A couple of years ago we were pulling a practical joke on Tom, and we had him going. We were playing in Tampa Bay, and it was a deal involving the number of matches you had hidden. Well, right before the game Tom told me he had stayed up most of the night trying to figure out the joke, and he couldn't. I explained it to him, and he said: "You son of a bitch" and he went out and played a great game. I don't know if he played so well because he was mad at me or mad at Tampa Bay. I think it was really just that Tom loves football so much. He is the ultimate player.

Dan Reeves,
Denver Broncos coach

ACKNOWLEDGMENTS

When I was playing football as a kid on 121st Street in Cleveland, I never imagined that someday I'd play in the NFL or the Pro Bowl or the Super Bowl. And when I was reading sports books about my athletic heroes while I was growing up, I never thought that someday I'd write one. Just goes to show you there's hope for all of us.

To Shari Lesser Wenk, who wanted this book, whether we won or lost, and had faith in the project.

To Woody Paige for his editorial assistance. He convinced me I had a story to tell and helped me tell it.

To Jim Saccamono, the director of media relations for the Broncos, and his staff, who provided me with a wealth of information.

To Gisela Billmayer for being my crutch and so often allowing me to lean on her.

To Buddy Martin, Joe Sanchez, Michael Knisely, and John McGrath of *The Denver Post*, and to B. G. Brooks and Dick Connor of *The Rocky Mountain News*, and to the other writers whose accounts filled in the memory gaps. And to the rest of the media people in Denver, and particularly Steve Alvarez, who were always fair to me.

To Broncos owner Pat Bowlen and coach Dan Reeves, who lent their support.

To my coaches, Joe Collier and Myrel Moore, who were always there when I needed them.

To all my teammates, past and present, especially the linebackers.

And to the fans, who made my career in Denver so rewarding and so special.

Thank you. I hope I've given something back.

T.J.,
Morrison, Colorado
March 1987

"I am in earnest—I will not equivocate—I will not excuse—I will not retreat a single inch—and I will be heard!"

William Lloyd Garrison

"Imagine that some drunken maniac has just run your car off the road and killed your wife and child. Think of how angry you are at him. That's the attitude I want you to have about your opponent when you go out and play the game."

John Ralston

"Mojo go to Oakland, walk on hot coals."

Tom Jackson

BLITZ

AN AUTOBIOGRAPHY

EX LIBRIS
PEGASUS

BLITZ (blits), n.: A defensive play used in passing situations when a defensive back or a linebacker rushes in a surprise attack in an attempt to sack the quarterback or force him to hurry his pass.

1
RHAPSODY IN ORANGE: THE STUFF DREAMS ARE MADE OF

EX LIBRIS
PEGASUS

Once upon a halftime in the Super Bowl we led 10–9.

Not half bad.

Yeah.

The Denver Broncos had been around for just over a quarter of a century, and I had been around for more than half those years, and we had been around together, and what goes around comes around, and here we were ahead of The Almighty New York Giants. Around and around we go, and where we stop, nobody knows.

John Elway had run on the Giants, and he had passed on the Giants, and our defense had shut down the Giants. The game shouldn't even have been that close. We should have been up 17–9 or 20–9 or more. We were dominating a team that had been favored to blow us completely out of the Super Bowl.

The only problem was that I was hurt.

Well, maybe not the only problem.

We came out of the locker room charged up for the third quarter. Thirty more minutes to become Champions of the World.

The loudspeakers were blaring that awful song "New
York, New York," and it only made us more determined.
At halftime we had formulated our strategy. We were
kicking off to the Giants to start the second half. If we
kept them from scoring, got good field position, and
scored another touchdown, we'd have them right where
we wanted them. The Giants would be devastated.

But that's not quite how it worked out.

New York returned the kickoff to the 37-yard line. As
I watched from the sideline on a bad knee, the Giants
quickly and efficiently marched down the field—Joe
Morris for three yards, a Phil Simms pass completion,
Morris once more, Simms passing again. Finally,
Simms hit tight end Mark Bavaro for a 13-yard touch-
down pass. If I had been in there, I would have pre-
vented it.

New York led 16–10.

The sun was getting ready to fall into the nearby
Pacific Ocean, and the sky was fading from blue to
gray. There was a chill and an uncertainty in the air,
and 100,000 people in the Super Bowl and millions
around the world waited and wondered.

And then . . .

Elway threw three incomplete passes, and we punted
back to the Giants.

Morris was stopped for no gain, and Simms was off
target on two passes. They punted to us.

Back and forth. Neither side with an advantage. The
third quarter ended with the Giants still ahead 16–10.

One of Elway's passes was intercepted early in the
fourth quarter, but the Giants fumbled back to us at
midfield. We picked up a first down, but Sammy
Winder was dropped for a three-yard loss, and Mark
Jackson couldn't hang on to an Elway pass. On third
down Elway scrambled short of the first down, and we
punted again.

The Giants struck three times at the heart of our
defense and came up a yard short. They punted back.

The chess match continued. Time was running out.

Elway threw to Vance Johnson for 20 yards, then to Steve Watson for another 14. But a draw play got only 2 yards, and a screen pass was good for only 3 more. John's third-down pass, a surprise—a bomb, 55 yards down the field—just slid off the fingertips of the diving Jackson. We punted with 4:18 left. We had to stop them one more time.

Simms bootlegged right for 12 yards to the 47, then gave to Morris for another 5. They were in our territory. Ottis Anderson carried for 3, then Morris for another 6. But instead of keeping it on the ground, Simms threw a short pass to Bavaro, and he rumbled down to our 32 at the two-minute warning.

That's enough.

I tore off the ice bag taped to my leg, went to Dan Reeves, and yelled: "I'm going in!"

Before the coach could deny me, I was on the field.

The crowd went crazy.

Joe Morris started on a counter to my side. First test. I used my patented halo spinner—spinning off the tackle to the inside—to get free, and I hit Morris high, and Rulon Jones took him down. No gain. Morris tried to kick me. "Do that again, you little asshole, and I'll rip your heart out," I said while pointing at him.

"I'll come at you again, dirtball," Morris said.

There was no pressure. Pressure is what you put on yourself.

Second down. Morris off left tackle. Nothing there. I got him again. "You can't take me," I said. Morris grabbed me by the jersey. "This time."

The play in the trenches was tough, especially on a senior citizen like me. Suddenly I felt like what I was, the oldest linebacker in the National Football League. I was grunting and grinding and grinning. The Super Bowl.

Third down.

I came on a blitz.

There's a song called "There Is Nothing Like a Dame."

But I'll tell you the truth: there is nothing like a blitz. A woman is a woman, but a blitz is a big play. I read once that the blitz was born on December 1, 1957, when the San Francisco 49ers shocked the New York Giants with the maneuver. However, I trace the blitz back to Don "Red" Ettinger, who played for the Giants in 1949. He was normally an offensive guard, but filled in at linebacker one game. In that one game, on third and long Ettinger rushed from his linebacker spot and shocked everybody, including his own teammates. The result was a sack. After the game everyone wanted to know what Red was doing out there on the field. He said: "I was just doggin' the quarterback a little." For years, the blitz was known as, you guessed it, the "Red Dog."

Of course, the blitz was really born in World War II. The Germans abandoned the preconceived notions of defense—the "D," as it were—and developed the *blitz-krieg*, a rapid advance into enemy territory using tanks, motorized infantry, and aircraft, successful because of the element of surprise.

That's what the blitz is about. The Germans, the Giants, and the 49ers had invented the blitz, and I perfected it.

And here I was using the blitz against the same Giants, about 30 years later, in the biggest game of my life.

I feel like I'm a great blitzer because of my speed and my size, and, yes, my intelligence. The blitz always has been my strength. It can turn a game around. But you've got to know when and where to use it. Sometimes the call will come in from the bench. My position is weakside linebacker, which is what we call Wanda. So the call would be "Wanda shoot, cover zero." That simple. Wanda shoot. I'm blitzing.

When you blitz, you have no idea if you'll make it to the quarterback. It's a race, a challenge. You don't know you'll get there until you get there. That's why you see so much enthusiasm after a sack of the quarterback. Sometimes you don't realize he still has the ball.

Most of the time you're too late. And if you do make it, you're stretching, diving, grabbing at the very last moment. It's you and the quarterback, man to man. Quarterbacks know you're coming. They can see you. They can hear you, especially on artificial turf. Sometimes they just sense you're there.

It was time to blitz Phil Simms.

The whole stadium stood still when Simms dropped back. He was looking for Bavaro on the right side. I hit him just as he cocked the ball in his right hand. The ball popped loose. My God, Tom. Pick it up. I grabbed for the ball. I couldn't get it. One of the Giants pushed me aside and reached for it, but I regained my balance just as the ball bounced up.

I had the precious ball in my hands. I started running as hard and as fast as I could on a gimpy leg. The pain was severe, but no way was I going to let it stop me. I could hear 100,000 voices amid the din.

I thought about 14 years with the Broncos, 22 years of organized football, the years of playing on 121st Street. This was what it was all about, the culmination of a career.

I scored.

I was engulfed. Somebody poured a bucket of Gatorade over me. I was carried off the field. MVP in the Super Bowl. World Champion. The theme from *Rocky*. What a way to retire.

Rich Karlis kicked the extra point, and we won the Super Bowl 17–16.

And then . . .
I woke up.

It was the morning of the Super Bowl, January 25, 1987.

A beautiful morning.

And if dreams were hopes, the Broncos would be riding high in the Super Bowl.

"Everybody knows that T.J. is one of the greatest people around, but I don't think anybody knows how much he's helped me since I came to Denver, especially in my rookie year. I was really going through some tough times then, and Tom was always there. He was always positive with me, always upbeat. He really encouraged me and helped me stay on an even keel through all those difficulties. It's always nice to have him around doing what he does best—play football."

John Elway,
Denver Broncos quarterback

2
IT WAS A DARK AND STORMY NIGHTMARE

EX LIBRIS
PEGASUS

We led 10–9 at halftime.

We lost 39–20.

A tale of two halves. It was the best of times and the worst of times.

We were beaten in the Super Bowl, *and* I got hurt, the worst possible scenario that could have happened. I wished I could go into the shower, find Bobby Ewing, and learn it was all a nightmare.

Forget the dreams.

I'll always believe that if I hadn't injured my knee, I would have made the difference. I just know I would have come up with a big play. But I didn't, and we didn't, and the New York Giants won Super Bowl XXI in 1987 at the Rose Bowl.

So be it.

But it still hurts so bad.

It had felt so good when the game started.

I had waited nine years since we lost the Super Bowl to Dallas in New Orleans, and I figured this was my last chance. I wanted to make the most of it.

I called the coin toss at midfield; we won, and we got the ball. All week long the Giants said they would stop John Elway from scrambling. On the very first play of the game he scrambled for 10 yards. Way to go, John.

Eight plays, four minutes, 45 yards, field goal. Three to nothing, Broncos. This is what it's all about.

The Giants come out throwing, a change from their usual game plan. They shift tight end Mark Bavaro to my side every play, trying to catch us off balance. Simms said later that he wanted to throw early because we would be in a man coverage, protecting against the run. He was right; we were wrong.

On the very first play I blitz Simms and knock him down. I get there maybe a half-step late, and I give him a pretty good crack. I'm here, Phil. Hello, welcome to the Super Bowl. I had a good feeling because of that play. If I can get in there like that so early, then the next time I've got a good shot of doing some damage.

Bavaro is penalized for holding me—for the second time. He got away with the first. But the Giants are moving.

And I'm injured. The third time Bavaro holds, he twists me around, and another player, I have no idea who, hits my knee. The same knee I've hurt before.

I limped off because we were going into X coverage, extra defensive backs, and the Giants went on to score. I figured I'd just gotten dinged, and I'd be back in soon enough. Rub some dirt on the leg and go on.

We failed to score, and the Giants got the ball again. I sat out the series while Kenny Woodard played. The Giants were stopped, and we got it going again.

John threw to Sammy Winder for 13 yards, then hit Orson Mobley and Winder again on a screen. Harry Carson threw Sammy down late out of bounds and picked up a personal foul. Lawrence Taylor said something he shouldn't have, and suddenly we had another 30 yards on penalties. First and goal at the Giants' six-yard line. On third and goal John pulled off a brilliant quarterback draw, and we were ahead 10–3.

I went back out on the field in the second quarter. We'd had an opportunity to move ahead 17–3, with first down on the Giants' one, but couldn't score, and Rich Karlis missed the field goal.

Dammit. You can't miss those opportunities against a good defense. And dammit. The pain was awful. I would try to shake it off, but on first down, I picked up Morris coming out of the backfield, and I knew it was all over. I couldn't move. I grabbed my leg and pulled up. It felt like someone had shot me in the knee.

T.J. was finished.

I was damaged goods. It turned out to be a partially torn ligament. There was a burning sensation, but the pain in my body couldn't compete with the pain in my mind. I looked up at the clock as the trainers were helping me off the field. With 6:40 left in the second quarter, was my career over?

Can you believe it? All the years, and all that work, all those dreams, and the Broncos' holler guy, the most inspirational, Mr. Excitement, stuck on the sidelines, helpless.

The rest of the game was an eerie kaleidoscope.

John completed a pass to Clarence Kay, but the officials ruled it incomplete. They couldn't find a replay that was conclusive. Later on, when they did, it showed that Kay *had* caught the ball. The mistake was a big one, because on the very next play George Martin trapped John in the end zone for a safety: 10–9.

Karlis misses another field goal . . . Halftime . . . Doctors say I can't play . . . I want to cry, but we're ahead by a point . . . Come on, guys . . . The Giants go right down the field for a touchdown. 16–10 . . . The biggest play of the game. On fourth down and one at their 46-yard line, the Giants go into punt formation, but we know they aren't punting. Our regular defense stays on the field. Then Jeff Rutledge moves under center. He looks at the sideline and gets a nod from coach Bill Parcells. He shouts out: "Check, roll tide." Then he takes the ball and wedges into the right side of the offensive line for a first down. We knew they were going to do that. I should have been there to stop it . . . They keep the ball and score . . . One fake punt really changes things . . . We're stopped . . . New York gets a field goal: 19–10 . . . Not out of reach . . . We punt once again . . . Giants are unstoppable, and it's painful to watch . . . Interception . . . Giants score again, 33–10 . . . We get a field goal—too little, too late—and it's out of hand, 33–13 . . . But they score again. Get it over with. We score . . . John Elway and I embrace on the sideline and console each other . . . They celebrate. End of the game. I hobble as fast as I can to the locker room.

Even when it was 26–10, I was still fairly confident that we would win. I remember what we did in Cleveland when we went 98 yards in the closing moments to snatch the victory. I knew we had the firepower to do it if we got after it. We would score a couple of touchdowns, stop the Giants, Rich would kick a field goal in the closing seconds, and we would win by a point, 27–26. Our first Super Bowl victory, triumphant. The most exciting Super Bowl finish in history, and I could announce right there at midfield that I was retiring.

Unfortunately, that's not what happened that Sunday at the Rose Bowl. When they made it 33–10, it was over. I'm an optimistic person, but I'm not totally stupid. You might come back and beat Tampa Bay in a preseason game from a 23-point deficit, but not the Giants. That's a great football team. And there was nothing I could do about it.

The early reports were that I had a sprained knee. If it had been a sprain, I would have figured a way to get back in there. The idea of taking a shot crossed my mind, but even that wouldn't have helped. I would have just fallen on my face.

In the locker room I didn't want to take off my
uniform. I just wanted to sit and be alone. But the
writers gathered.

"What do you think?" one reporter asked.

"I think I shouldn't have gotten out of bed today."

Another reporter came along.

"Tom, what do you think?"

"I think I should go see a doctor."

I was fighting back the tears.

EX LIBRIS
PEGASUS

"Tom was a leader up front in high school, and a hardworking, self-motivated guy on his own. He was a fun-loving guy—a good person to be around—who gave me only one problem the whole time. He was hurt one game and was on the sidelines and did so much screaming the other team got upset—and beat the crap out of us."

Bob Harrison,
Jackson's high school football coach

3
THOMAS JACKSON III'S DAYS OF GOLDEN MEMORIES

Men are not supposed to cry. But I learned how when my mother died. I. was only 13, and we were just beginning to get to know each other. She never even saw me play football. I still miss her, especially when times are bad, like after the Super Bowl. If you think I'm tough, you should have seen my mother. Katie Lane Jackson was a strong lady. She had to be. She came out of the dirt of Mississippi.

My grandparents on my mother's side lived in a small town on the Mississippi–Tennessee border. Michigan City. Sounds like a big, northern city, but there wasn't much around Michigan City except farmers. I used to hear from my older relatives about the racial prejudice my mother had to put up with in the South. I guess it was just something she wanted to forget. So, unlike Alex Haley, I haven't traced my family's roots back to Africa. All I know is that my father was from St. Louis, my mother from Mississippi.

I've seen the pictures of Grandpa Tim and Grandma

31

Lilly down in Mississippi, and I can imagine life
couldn't have been too easy in the South for blacks
back then. I know that racism affected my father,
though to this day he has never brought it up. Once,
when I was a kid, I was going through his drawers, and
I found a clipping from an old *Life* magazine. It talked
about a young black man being lynched in the South
just because he talked to a white girl. I don't know why
my father kept that article, but I sat there and read it,
and that was the first time I ever really had heard
anything about prejudice toward blacks.

My father—Thomas Jackson, Jr.; I'm the third—
fought in Europe during World War II and went to
Memphis, Tennessee, after the war and met my mother.
They got married and moved to Cleveland in the late
1940s, a year before I was born. They just didn't want to
deal with the things going on in the South. My dad got
a job painting water meters, and he had that job until
he retired. Never missed a day of work. Never com-
plained about his job and took a lot of pride in his work.
He's 78 now, and he'll be alive when I'm gone.

Cleveland was a growing, bustling city while I was
growing up. We lived in southeast Cleveland, 121st
Street. Real people. Rows of two-story brick houses and
three-foot hedges. It was a lot different from Denver,
but I didn't know about places like Denver. In Denver,
people are always out by the pool, tanning themselves,
playing volleyball or something. In Cleveland we never
saw any of that. Nobody worked on a tan, certainly not
the blacks. We worked all week and rested all weekend.
It was like, "Don't bother me, and I won't bother you."
When I came to Denver, it was a real culture shock. I'm
sure that if I had spent the rest of my life in Cleveland
I would have been a totally different person.

If you say you're black and from Cleveland, people
think you must have come from the ghetto. But I don't
have a hard-luck, ghetto story for you. I didn't sleep in a
room with 11 kids. I didn't starve. I wasn't thrown in jail

at six. We lived in a nice, middle-class neighborhood, and my father has never moved. A lot of the people who grew up on that street are still there. There are guys I went to nursery school, elementary school, junior high, and high school with, and they've never left 121st Street. Never wanted to, never had a reason. And a lot of them are doing exactly what they've always been do-ing—hanging out at the shoeshine shop or doing noth-ing. We all pretty much had the same values when we started out. Some got out. A lot didn't. Some became winos and junkies. One of my friends, Willie, became a heroin addict, robbed a place, and shot a cop. There must be a fine line between turning out OK and ending up in jail. I'm not smart enough to know what the difference is.

When I was little, my street was my whole life. Everybody knew what everybody else in the neighbor-hood was doing. If someone died or went crazy or got drunk or left his wife, we knew about it immediately. There were little old ladies who sat and looked out their windows all day. That was their job, to know what was going on and to tell everybody else. We'd have block parties, and everybody'd get involved. Like Christmas, the street would light up. And when I was growing up, Halloween was the greatest day of the year. None of that stuff you hear about today, people putting razor blades in apples or acid in candy.

About the craziest thing we did as kids was to sit through a horror movie 10 or 11 times the same day. I'll never forget the only time I ever stole anything. It was a bag of M&Ms I took from Kroger's. I did it on a dare and took them home, but I couldn't eat them. I was afraid the FBI was going to come nab me at any moment.

I don't think I ever considered going bad. I was a build-a-treehouse kind of kid. That was because of the influence of my mother and father and my sister, Barbara. Actually, Barbara was my stepsister. She had a different father, and she was 10 years older than I, but we were typical brother and sister. And she kept me in line. Our relationship really changed after our mother died. She tried to take on that role for me. She couldn't be my mother, but Barbara and I became a lot closer, especially as we got older. After my mother died so abruptly, Barbara moved back in and tried to fill that space. But I had to grow up fast.

People say I never stop talking on the football field. Well, that started very young. In elementary school, notes came home all the time saying: "Tom won't shut up in the classroom. Does not always stop when told to." I'm a talker.

But I was never much trouble. Mostly what we did was play football in the street. We didn't have beautiful parks and playgrounds nearby, so we used the curbs as out-of-bounds. We had some of the greatest games in history on 121st Street. Teams would come from 123rd or 127th and challenge us, and it couldn't get any better than that.

Even though our house had three bedrooms, my sister and I shared a room. My parents kept the other room as a guest bedroom. When my sister became a teenager, she finally begged them to let her have the middle bedroom. We were real tired of each other. The day she moved out of that bedroom was one of the happiest days of my life.

We always knew what the rules were in that house. And as long as I've lived, I've never cursed in that house. Once I got into trouble for saying the word *lie*. I called somebody in our backyard a liar, and my dad was standing in the kitchen and heard me. He really got on me for that. He always told me: "When you are in this house, you do as I say. When you're in your own house, you can do what you want." In fact, I reminded him of that statement when he came to my house for Thanksgiving last year. I had the stereo turned up slightly loud—well, *real* loud—and my dad told me to turn it down. I said: "Dad, do you remember saying that when I'm in my house I can do what I want to do? Well, I'm in my house now. We're here." But I turned down the stereo anyway.

My father is a good, strong man. He won't let anything get him down, and if something does, he won't show it. He had a ring given to him by my mom, a black onyx, that he let me wear to school every once in a while. We had "dress-up days," and that ring made me feel so important. It was too big for me, of course, so I wore tissue behind it to keep it from falling off. One day, I realized the ring was gone. I rushed to the principal and told him to close the doors, guard them, and search everyone. I had to have that ring back. I found out that's not the way life works. Well, I just couldn't tell my father. That Sunday morning when he got dressed for church, he told me: "Junior, go get my ring." I said: "Dad, I've got some really bad news for you. I've lost the ring." With the exception of my mom's death, I don't think I've ever really seen him that sad. He was devastated. My mom had given him that ring, and it meant so much to him. I always told myself that if I could ever give him something that would be close to that ring, I'd try to make it up to him.

So when we got to the Super Bowl the first time, I gave him my ring. It wasn't the champions' ring; it was for winning the AFC title. Maybe it eased my own mind. When I gave it to him, we both knew why.

My dad never threw the ball around with me—my mother did that—but he did take me to see the Cleveland Browns. When he'd announce that we were going to a Browns game, it was better than Christmas. We'd sit high up in those cold stands, in terrible seats, usually behind the poles. But it didn't matter. I ate the dogs, and I kept my eyes on Jim Brown. He was our man. J.B. You never heard his name when he was introduced because as soon as they said, "Number 32," the stadium went berserk. Nowadays when it's third and two, I see offenses like ours struggle to make a decision on what to do—like when we were on the one-yard line in the Super Bowl. In Cleveland when I was a kid, when it was third and two, there was no doubt who would get the ball. You didn't need to study the films. The people in the stadium knew. The people on the other team knew. The people listening to the radio knew. Jim Brown was going to get that football. He may have treated women miserably, and he may have gotten in trouble wrecking his car during the week, but on Sunday at one o'clock, J.B., Jim Brown, was a god in Cleveland. He was everything you wanted in a football player.

Like every other kid, I wanted to grow up to be Jim Brown. My father would send me down to the corner grocery for the paper every night, and I'd run through the snow between the cars and jump over the hedges, pretending I was Jim Brown. My father was a Browns fan until they traded Paul Warfield, and he said he would never go back to Cleveland Municipal Stadium as long as he lived. And he would have kept that promise if I hadn't become a pro football player. Actually, when I came back to Cleveland the first time to play, I think it was kinda tough for him to come out because he had promised he would *never* go back. He had to justify it by saying he was coming to see me, not the Browns.

My father never said much about my playing football. He wasn't much with praise. When we played our first playoff game, against Pittsburgh in Denver, I flew him out. I had two interceptions and recovered a fumble inside the Pittsburgh 10-yard line, and I like to think I had a lot to do with our winning the game. It was my best game ever. Afterward, my father was waiting in the dark outside Mile High Stadium. We got in the car, and he put his arm on mine and said: "Pretty good game." That's all he said, but that was enough. That was the best thing anybody ever said to me about the way I've played.

But my mom never saw me play, and that's my biggest regret. She was an incredible lady, the one everyone depended on to hold everything together. Whenever people in the church got sick, she took over their home, cooking the food and taking care of the family. But she made sure we had everything we needed. She had a job for a while, but she never missed a day of fixing our breakfast and being home to cook supper, too. We knew if she wasn't home, she was off doing something for somebody else.

She was never sick a day of her life—or, at least, she didn't show it—until I was 13. Then, five days later, she was gone. She had a headache one morning. It was the first time in my life she didn't cook me breakfast. When I came home that evening, she was still lying down. The next night I woke up in the middle of the night, and they were taking her off to the hospital. I never saw her alive again.

I had seen people who had had a stroke, and I knew she had had one. But because I was a kid, I couldn't go to the hospital, and later on that turned out to cause some real problems for me. She had been the focus of my life, and then she went away, and I didn't even get to talk to her about why she was going away. I didn't even get to say good-bye. I think it affected all my future relationships with women. Maybe that's the reason I've never been around another woman permanently. I don't want to lose someone else as abruptly as I lost my mother.

I couldn't accept it for a while. Months later, someone would call out to me, and I would think it was my mother. Or I would be walking down the street and see someone with the same physical features as my mother, and I would run to her, yelling that it was my mom. I always thought she would be coming home from the hospital.

One afternoon my father came home and said to my grandma: "Katie passed away about an hour ago." Very softly. I went upstairs and went to bed. I didn't cry. You weren't supposed to cry if you were a man. When I woke up, I thought I had dreamed it. But my sister came in, and I knew my mom had died. I began to cry. I've never stopped crying for my mother, I don't think.

She wanted to be buried back down south, where we have a family plot in Mississippi. I didn't want to look in the casket, but my father made me. I thought it was cruel at the time, but he was right. He wanted me to know that she was really dead. All the way down to Mississippi in the car all I could think about was that I hadn't been nice enough to my mother and hadn't done anything to make her really proud of me. I think I've spent a lot of my life trying to make it up to her.

After the funeral, I became real bitter. Everyone had gathered at the relatives' house, and they started eating. It's a southern tradition to eat a lot after a funeral. The Irish drink, and the southerners drown their sorrow in potatoes and gravy and fried chicken. I couldn't understand it. They were eating and talking and laughing, and my mother had just been buried. I had problems dealing with that for a long time.

I was depressed for months. I didn't say or do much. I withdrew. You see, I could talk with my mother. They talk now about the communication between parents and kids. Well, at a time when I needed my mother to be there, she wasn't. No one talked to me about the facts of life or any of that stuff. I had to learn a lot on my own from then on. I created a lot of pressure for myself to be something special for my mom.

I got the feeling I could be special when I was a little kid, seven or eight, and we went out to an amusement park called Euclid Beach, a place with roller coasters and other rides and a park and everything. They had a big Memorial Day weekend, and one of the events was a race. You had to duck-walk for part of it and come back on your hands and heels. There were maybe 150 kids who were in the race, but I won it. The prize was a pack of balloons and a 45 record.

I always look back at that moment as the first sign I could be pretty good in athletics. I think my competitive spirit started with that package of balloons—you could actually win something for being faster than everybody else. Of course, what really prepared me were those games in the street and the basketball in the backyards. We had some gifted athletes on 121st, and they pushed me. You had to be tough. I didn't like to fight, but sometimes I was forced to.

To me, being tough is overcoming fear. Every time you go into a big game in this league, you have some fear. Don't let anyone tell you otherwise. They're fearful that they're going to get beat. They're afraid of getting hurt. They fear that the other guy will be better than they are. And the way they get over that fear is by being tough. What I really learned in the neighborhood is that Grantland Rice, the sportswriter, was right. It's not always whether you win or lose. That's a lesson a lot of coaches and ball players and fans never learn. If you fight a guy and you fight well, more than likely, the guy will leave you alone. He doesn't want to fight you every day and deal with that hassle. He'll find someone else to pick on. The same thing is true in the rest of your life. If you put up a good fight, people will respect you, and they won't go on trying to beat on you anymore. When you get to the level of professional football, everyone is a good athlete. They wouldn't be there if they weren't. So you better be satisfied that you can't always be the best, and you can't always win. Fans don't understand why sometimes we aren't more upset when we lose. Sometimes you just aren't good enough, no matter what you do. You have to find some other satisfaction, like knowing that you'll play harder than anybody else. My mother instilled that in me.

After she died I didn't do much for a while, but one day I was sitting in the park, watching a bunch of guys play football. I had never played organized ball before. It was the team from John Adams High School, which I was about to attend. I watched for a while, and I liked what I saw. I felt that if I played football, it would be a way to help get over my mother's death. It would give me a release for the pain I couldn't get over, and maybe it was a way for me to show her that I could accomplish something good. So I went over to the coach and asked for a tryout.

The next day I got a uniform, and I found out right away I wasn't very good. In fact, I was awful. I told the coach I was a running back because I wanted to be just like Jim Brown. The first two times I carried the football in practice I fumbled it. The coach told me to get over there with the defense, and that's how I became a linebacker. And it was the end of my running back career. Who knows? If I hadn't fumbled, maybe I would have been Jim Brown or Gale Sayers. But as a running back I wouldn't even have made it to college ball.

In my sophomore year I never even got to dress for a game. At the end of the week the coach would always name the starting team and the guys who were going to dress. I was never told to dress. There were 70 guys on the team, and 65 got to dress. I was in the other five. That shows you how bad I was. It was embarrassing. I sat in the stands. I didn't play that year because I didn't have the ability. I didn't know technique, and I was still pretty small then. I'm still pretty small, I guess. I had absolutely no polish. I would be blasting the guard, but I had no idea how to get to the ball carrier. I didn't know what to do or where the football was. I still had to figure out what the game was all about. So I watched for a whole season and decided I was going to get serious about it. During the off-season, my best friend, Michael Cunningham, and I worked on our game and lifted weights in the garage. When I came back the next year, I had some polish, and my game started to develop. I had gone from 165 to 185, and I was starting to wrestle, too. I was OK my junior year, but by the time I was a senior I was a player. During that summer I had gone down south to Mississippi and stayed with my grandparents, and my body matured. I lost a lot of baby fat, and I learned the meaning of hard work, being out in the fields picking okra. One thing I knew, I didn't want to pick vegetables the rest of my life. College became a lot more important.

I knew that I was becoming more than an average player because I had led the team in tackles and made an interception. And that's also when I started to become a bit more vocal. Once, I was standing on the sidelines, hurt. I wanted to be in that game so bad I began screaming at the other team, some nasty things. Well, they got even madder and beat us bad. Our coach just glared at me. But I couldn't keep my mouth shut. To me, talking and getting after people is what it's all about. I remember intercepting a pass, my first one, and running it back about 60 yards against Glenville. I had eyes for a touchdown, and we were ahead about three touchdowns already. I got knocked out of bounds right by Glenville's bench. Their guys all ran over and started spitting on me. That was the most memorable thing that happened to me in high school. I never forgot being treated like that. Nobody was ever going to get away with that again.

Martin Luther King, Jr., died on my birthday, April 4, 1968. I came home from the playground dribbling my basketball and getting excited about a party we were going to have. I walked into the house, and you could feel death. There was something about it I'll never forget. My father looked at me and said Martin Luther King had been killed. Everybody was stunned. He had meant so much to us. We had no party. We just sat there. It was one more time I felt death very close to me. On the football team my senior year one of the players got sick and went over to sit under a tree. Then he just fell over and died. I think I was becoming hardened to death.

I was named captain of the team my senior year, and I was surprised that I started to get letters from colleges

asking me to come visit. I had only one aspiration at the
time: to play at Ohio State. There wasn't another school
in the country I wanted to go to. Growing up and
playing football in Ohio, there are just two places you
want to go—either you go to Ohio State, or you go to
Michigan and come back and beat Ohio State. So I
thought if I had a really great senior year I would be a
cinch for a scholarship at Ohio State. It was for sure
that I wasn't going to get an academic scholarship, so
my only chance to go to college was to make it in sports.

I was thrilled when the assistant coach from Ohio
State finally came to visit. This was going to be the best
day of my life. My dream of playing for the Buckeyes
would be fulfilled. Playing for Woody Hayes. He was
the king. Well, this assistant, whose name I have wisely
forgotten, took one look at me and said to me: "You
don't have the size to play linebacker in the Big Ten. I'm
being honest with you." It was one of those "don't call
us" things. That was it. Shattered in a minute. Ohio
State didn't want me. They thought I was a scrawny,
185-pound, 5-foot-10 linebacker. I was ruined.

I could have gone in one of two ways then. I could
have accepted what he said, but instead I chose to get
pissed off and prove to him and everyone else at Ohio
State that I could play linebacker and make it happen.
After that, it didn't particularly matter what school I
went to. I just wanted an opportunity to show the world
what Tom Jackson could do.

Not many schools were interested because of my size.
But Lee Corso came up personally from Louisville.
Although he doesn't know this, he recruited me the first
two minutes he talked to me. I had talked to a lot of
coaches before then, and they had told me about their
schools and their programs and all that routine. I had it
down perfectly. "This is a picture of our school. Here's
one of our weight room and our dorm. We expect to go
to a bowl game, and if we can get so-and-so and so-and-
so and you, we can have a great football team, and

you'll love our team and our school, blah, blah, blah."
Corso sat down and introduced himself, and I asked
him, as usual, to tell me a little bit about his school.
He said: "I can't tell you anything about this school. I
just got the job a few weeks ago. All I can tell you is I got
about six guys from this area I want to play for me, and
if I can get them and the other guys from around the
country I want, I believe we can turn this program
around." Louisville, I found out later, had been thinking about giving up football but hired Corso instead
and gave it one last chance. I thought to myself: "This
guy is so honest he's the kind of coach you want to play
for."

I went there for one weekend to look around the
campus. I had a talk with the coaches, and then I got
involved in a softball game/beer keg party. Every time
you won, your team sat out and drank a half keg of
beer. What I remember is that I passed out between
third base and home when I was running. I woke up
that evening, and Horace Jones, who later played for the
Raiders, was packing me into a car—I was sick as a
dog—and taking me downtown to a hotel. The Platters
were singing, and my head was spinning. But I thought
about how much I was going to like this college life. The
next morning I told Coach Corso I wanted to go to
school at Louisville.

I actually had more offers, about 20, from colleges for
wrestling scholarships. I enjoyed wrestling even more
than football because it was all yourself. You couldn't
depend on anyone else to bail you out or get the handoff
or run the right route. You did it, or you got beat. It was
one on one. I got all the way to the state finals in
Columbus, until this brute just about killed me. I had
no chance whatsoever. He threw me around like a
dishrag for five or six minutes, and I went on home.

I was a better wrestler than I was a football player,
but I compared my future in football and my future in
wrestling and picked football. The only wrestlers I saw

were the pro wrestlers. My father took me down to the auditorium to see those guys a couple of times, and I loved watching Bo Bo Brazil against Fritz Von Erich, but I knew I didn't want to end up making money that way. At least I hoped not. But I think my wrestling experience made it possible for me to play pro football. Because I wasn't the biggest guy, I had to learn ways to beat bigger guys. I had to be quicker and smarter and have more moves. I think that's really how I learned to blitz.

None of the schools offered me secret money or cars or anything. I've heard about the money some people get when they decide on a school. I can say truthfully that nobody ever gave me anything under the table. I guess that shows you what they thought of my ability to play. Wait. I'm wrong. An assistant coach did give me a bonus for signing. On the national signing date he picked up the five players from Cleveland who were going to Louisville and took us out for a steak dinner, then bowling, and then to a Cleveland Indians game. So Louisville must have spent about 20 bucks on me.

I was off to play college football and show Ohio State and everybody else that I could make it.

EX LIBRIS
PEGASUS

"When I first met him, Tom was like an altar boy—no swearing, no drinking. He didn't know anything. He's still a lot like an altar boy, except when you get him on a football field. I think Tom always wanted a bunch of brothers. We became roommates later, but my sophomore year I was living with another guy in the dorm, and Tom would come to our room every night and sleep in the middle of the floor."

Rick Howard,
Jackson's best friend

4
BRAVE NEW WORLD

My four years at Louisville were spectacular. College and I fit together well. Boola, boola.

It was an interesting time to be in college. Students were protesting the Vietnam War. I had friends who took over the administration building. And if I had been drafted, I would have been in Vietnam. My dad would have made sure of that. He wouldn't have accepted a son who went off to Canada to dodge the draft. I remember sitting there the night they had the draft lottery, and my number was real low—I was fortunate. I imagine Vietnam was worse than playing against the Raiders.

So I was able to enjoy college and not worry about going off to Asia and dying. And we were into good times. But when I was a freshman, we sure had a rotten football team. Back then, freshmen weren't allowed to play, and I watched as Memphis State won the Missouri Valley Conference championship, beating us 69–19. This was a long way from Ohio State. Toward the end of the game Coach Corso started waving a white flag at the Memphis State side, but the Memphis fans were screaming for their team to get 70 points. The next day Corso let the freshmen scrimmage against the varsity starters. We beat them 21–0. The next year he started 19 sophomores, and we won the conference championship.

I had dated a girl in high school who went on to Ohio State. Since it was so close, about 200 miles, I traveled back and forth. The more I learned about the school, the more I was impressed. Since our freshman team at Louisville played only five games, we had a lot of weekends off. If the varsity was on the road, we'd drive up to Columbus for the weekend. Let's face it. I still wanted to be at Ohio State, to impress the people, to impress my girlfriend. I decided to transfer.

When I was named Most Valuable Freshman, I sat Lee Corso down in his office one day and told him I wanted to go to Ohio State, that I could play Big Ten football. He told me if that's what I wanted, he would help me in any way he could. But the next day he gave this speech to the team about committing yourself to something and sticking with it, and building character didn't always depend on where you were competing, but how you were competing. In essence, he was telling me I wasn't going anywhere.

Those years, 1969 to 1973, were tumultuous times in the history of this country. For one thing, I realized that there were people out there who believed that blacks were "different." I didn't have any perception that defined the difference between blacks and whites. Maybe there would be something on the news about the way blacks were being treated someplace, but, from what I knew, all kids were the same. I went to schools that were totally integrated. I had white and black teachers and white and black friends, and I didn't realize anyone was thinking about me in terms of color. The reality hit me in college. All of a sudden, something happened. A bunch of us went up to a college bar in

Louisville, the Zanzibar. When we went in, a group of black ball players, there was tension right away. I thought it was because we were college football players. Shows you how immature I still was. They didn't want us there because we were black. The cops were called, and they told us to go back to campus. We did, but I knew then we were being told to go away because we were black, and the people in the bar didn't like us because we were black. That was the first time I really experienced prejudice.

And the sexual revolution was going on. When I first went to Louisville, we had specific dorm hours, and you couldn't visit a girl in her dorm. By the time I got out of school you could go live with a woman in her dorm if you wanted to.

And then there was Lee Corso. He was incredible. I don't think he ever got the credit he deserved as a coach because of the weird things he did. My favorite story is about the time we played Tulsa. It was around Thanksgiving, and we'd been lacking enthusiasm that week. Everybody was thinking how nice it would be to go home and spend Thanksgiving with our families. Lee must have understood because when we went to the dining hall one morning for breakfast he had this turkey up on the head table. A live turkey! He didn't say anything about it. Game day, and sure enough, in the locker room, there's the turkey. Corso explains that he has a bet with the Tulsa coach, Vince Gibson. If Tulsa wins the game, they get the turkey, and they're going to kill it and eat it for Thanksgiving. If we win the game, we release the turkey. He even had a name for the turkey, George. As we filed out of the locker room he made each one of us pat the turkey on the head. Then that turkey led us out on the field. You should have seen what that did to us. We whipped Tulsa that day—shut 'em out, in fact. That was the thing about Lee. We were nothing my freshman year, but by my senior year we were ranked 11th in the nation.

I never heard anything about steroids. My one experience with drugs in college was enough. My junior year I got hurt against Dayton. I took a tremendous lick on the knee and was carried off the field on a stretcher. The doctor didn't even ask me about the leg in the locker room. He just gave me a shot of novocaine cortisone. Big dose. Long needle. I didn't even know what it was. All I know is that five minutes later, my leg, which I had thought would have to be amputated, felt brand new. Not only did it not hurt, but it felt better than it ever had before in my whole life. It felt better than my other leg. I was King Kong. I thought they had discovered some wonder drug. So I came back out, and I played, and I played good, and then I played great, and on the way home on the bus, we were sitting there talking and laughing because we had won the game. And I started to feel this twinge in my leg. The twinge became a pain, and the pain became excruciating, and I was on the floor of the bus, crawling and screaming. I was dragging my leg around in the aisle while the doctor gave me more painkillers. One drug led to another. And I dealt with that all the way home. My leg never was the same—not that season, not ever. It was a stark realization of what other people were willing to do to my body to get me to play football.

A lot of players have wised up in that area now. Very few players are willing to take those shots anymore. But here's the contradiction: the bigger the game, the more things you're willing to try or do to be in it. The standard line from trainers and doctors is that you're injured and it hurts, but you can play on this injury without hurting it more. They make it sound like you should be willing to play hurt because it can't get any worse. And then they say it's your decision to make. Of course, that decision is always going to be that you will play. Since you've been playing the game you've been brainwashed to believe that you must always play, or it's a sign that you're not tough. Plus, if you don't play, there's someone waiting to take your spot, and you may never get back out there again. So do it. Sacrifice your body. I've been hurt many times, dating back to college, and I was always so proud that most of the time I could overcome the pain and play. That makes me either tough or stupid. Or both. But you want to be in there, no matter the cost. You take a blow on the knee, and it hurts. Damn, it hurts. But it gets closer to game time, and you've watched the film, and you've gotten excited, and the adrenaline starts to flow, and you get out in front of 75,000 people, and suddenly the leg doesn't hurt anymore. The pain has gone away—at least, for three or four hours. Take four or five Ascription. Put some heat on the muscle. And play. Tomorrow night at 11 o'clock it's a different story. Yeah, a different story. That leg will kill you. You can't walk. You can't get out of bed. But there's no game to play and no 75,000 people watching. The pain returns.

I still have trouble convincing people that Louisville was ever the 11th-best team in the country one year. I tell them that, and they ask me what division. We went 9–1 my senior year. We hit a hot Tulsa team that had Drew Pearson, and they were the only team that beat us. Nowadays Louisville is spending millions of dollars trying to get the program going again, bringing in Howard Schnellenberger. But back then they didn't spend a dime. We played in the Fairgrounds Stadium, which was built for baseball. On one side were stands, and on the other side was I-65. It was always muddy, and they put down sawdust to try to soak up the water. After every play I had to pull wet sawdust out of my mouth. It surely was no Ohio State.

But things were falling into place for Tom Jackson. I got an off-season job at Louisville Cement Co. and spent the money as fast as I got it. I discovered sex. I bought a stereo. I asked my father for a car, and he said I would appreciate my first car more if I bought it. Ha. My grades were average, but we were winning on the football field. One day at a pep rally, Corso came in and announced the top 15 teams in the country. He named Alabama and Oklahoma and Texas and Ohio State and Southern Cal and Arkansas, and then he paused and said: "No. 13, Louisville." We started clapping, and he said: "Let me read those teams again . . . Alabama and Oklahoma . . . and Louisville." We went nuts.

There was no doubt in my mind that I deserved to be a number one draft choice. But the computers were spitting out my size, and no way was I going to be a number one draft choice. How could a team tell the folks back home they had drafted a little linebacker in the first round? I was too young to understand the politics of the situation. A lot of times teams draft people who look good on paper, even if they're no good on the field. I read a couple of those scouting magazines that said: "Oh, if he was only two inches taller and 20 pounds heavier, Tom Jackson would be a superb player." Those statistics and those computers don't test heart and desire. That's where they come up short, and that's how mistakes are made. That's why free agents like Joe Rizzo and Bob Swenson and Steve Watson can make it, how a low-round draft pick like Karl Mecklenburg can become an All-Pro. The people who are supposed to know don't always know. The Broncos took a chance on Karl, and look what they have—one of the best defensive players in the league. You can't measure the intangibles.

Nevertheless, I was still very disappointed that I didn't go higher. The Dallas Cowboys told me they were going to draft me in the second round. I found out later the Cowboys tell all the players they're going to draft them in the second round. I was hoping I could go home to Cleveland and play in front of my friends and on the same field where Jim Brown and Leroy Kelly played. The Browns needed defensive help. One of their outside linebackers had retired. The last place I ever thought about was Denver, Colorado.

After the first couple of rounds of the draft I stopped paying attention. I was destroyed. I had been Missouri Valley Conference Player of the Year twice, and I had great stats. I could run a 4.5 40, great for a linebacker. I couldn't believe nobody wanted me. Then I got a call from Fred Gehrke, who was the assistant general manager of the Broncos, and he told me I had been picked in the fourth round. The first thing my roommate, Rick Howard, and I did was go find a map. I didn't even know where Denver was. I thought it was somewhere next to Salt Lake City. All I could think about was playing in snow and cold the rest of my life. I was miserable. Besides, I had never heard about Denver winning anything. The Denver Broncos? Who ever heard of the Broncos? They weren't ever on TV or in the playoffs. What the hell had gone wrong? Where were the Cowboys? I finally make it to pro football, but I end up with the Denver Broncos, of all teams.

About two weeks later I flew out to Denver for the first time to see the city and begin negotiations. My lawyer, John Knopf, who was also the attorney for the state of Kentucky, went with me. I had no idea what kind of money I was going to get. They probably could have given me a thousand dollars, and I wouldn't have known any better. Gehrke took me up in the mountains to his private club, and it was one of those perfect days in Colorado, about 60 degrees, blue skies, fantastic. We talked for a while, then I went back to Kentucky and returned a week or so later.

John and Fred go into a room and leave me sitting outside reading magazines. A little while later John comes out, and he has a contract. He tells me to sign. What do I know? I sign for $21,500, with a $15,000 bonus. They write me a check for $15,000. It's all the money in the world. These Broncos are giving me $15,000 to play football. I've made it. I'm in the big time. This is it. There's no higher I could go.

On the way home I made John pull that check out

three or four times. When we got there, he asked me who should keep the check. I told him I would keep the check. It was my money, and I would hold on to my money. My dad had taught me that much. John told me not to do anything foolish with the money. He knew I wanted a car—I had been walking all my life—and told me not to rush into anything. He would talk to his friends about getting me a good deal.

Well, a guy with $15,000 cash in his pocket don't need no deal and don't need nobody else to buy a car for him. A guy with $15,000 can buy his own car. So immediately I go to a Chevy dealership owned by a friend's dad. I look at these beautiful Monte Carlos, and they ask me if I want to test-drive one. I take out a colonial gold Monte Carlo with a black top and a sun roof and an eight-track tape deck. After all of three blocks, I wheel back to the showroom and tell the salesman that's what I want: I'll take it.

He wanted to know how I was going to pay for it. It was the proudest moment of my life. I announced: "Cash money." And I paid the sticker price. I got the car and drove back to Louisville and piled my friends in and went cruising. The next day John found out what I had done. He went back to that dealership and made them give me $2,000 of my money back. I have since learned that you don't pay the sticker price on a car, especially when you have cash. I was a little naive, but that was the first time I ever had money.

I thought I had made it. I loved Denver. I had money. I had a car. I had it all. Or so I thought. I still had a lot to learn. And training camp was about to teach me a few lessons.

"Tom Jackson's first year in the National Football League, woolly mammoths roamed the earth. It was the year they introduced the Statue of Liberty. It was the year they legalized the forward pass. Well, maybe he isn't quite that ancient, but Denver's Tom Jackson is the oldest living line-backer. Or at least the oldest one still in working condition. But he is still remarkably spry for a museum piece."

Bruce Keidan,
Pittsburgh Post-Gazette *columnist*

5
IN WHICH I RELATE THE STORY OF T.J. IN WONDERLAND

EX LIBRIS
PEGASUS

My whole life I had been told I was too small. And I was going to make sure nobody said that when I went to my first training camp with the Broncos. So I spent the summer eating everything in sight.

I reported at 235 pounds.

I felt like Shamu the Whale. It was the heaviest I've ever been.

The first day we had to run a mile and a half. I could barely make it, and I threw up for another three miles. Forget 235. In a few weeks I was back at 220, 218, where I belong.

But it was not a pleasant time.

It started when I met John Ralston, the coach. He started feeling my muscles, my biceps. I was trying to figure what kind of coach this was. I was wondering if he was queer. He said: "Hey, Tom Jackson. The fourth round has been a big round for us. We drafted Lyle Alzado in the fourth round." I was wondering, who the hell is Lyle Alzado? Does that mean nobody will know who I am, either? They showed the rookies the highlight film of the previous year—I guess to try to motivate us—and that's when I saw this wild man on defense. Lyle Alzado. Fourth round. Was I supposed to be the new wild man?

This was a team supposedly on the way up. Ralston had promised everybody that he would take the team to the Super Bowl. But in his first year, 1972, the Broncos finished 5–9. No Super Bowl.

The funny thing is that Ralston wasn't even supposed to be the coach. Gerald Phipps, the owner, had worked out an agreement with Bill Peterson to coach, but Peterson neglected to tell him he had already signed a contract with the Houston Oilers. This is the same Peterson who told his players in Houston: "I want you to remember one word and one word only—Super Bowl." Strange guy.

Ralston was strange, too. He came into the locker room one day and said: "Men, listen up. I want everybody to think for a minute. Name me one word that you can put in front of *ball* that doesn't have to do with sports." Obviously, John had been working on this speech for days to get us fired up, and he had looked up every possible word that has ball in it. Volleyball, football, baseball, and on and on. And he was getting ready to make some big point. But John Rowser, a defensive back, held up his hand and said very quietly: "*Meat*ball, Coach." Ralston looked at Rowser like he was going to kill him. Then he stormed out of the room.

And Rowser was traded.

Ralston spent most of his time talking about the Super Bowl—*two* words in Denver, two words we weren't familiar with. John had come from Stanford, where he and Jim Plunkett had taken the team to the Rose Bowl, twice. He was Mr. Positive. My rookie year, Ralston had index cards everywhere that said: "Win 10 games, lose 4, go to and win the Super Bowl." Nice try.

I wasn't thinking about the Super Bowl. I just wanted

to make the club. But I kept thinking I was going to get cut. And then I got hurt. We were training in California at Cal Poly, and in our very first scrimmage I got hit on the right knee. I collapsed on the field, and I heard the doctors say that was it. Torn cartilage. I looked up, and everybody acted like I had died. Knowing what I know now, that's what they were thinking. A rookie who hurts his knee might as well be shot and taken away. He's finished.

I packed my stuff to go to Denver for an operation, and I got in a cab with the team doctor, John Leidholt, to go to the airport. Tom Graham, who was the middle linebacker then, said as we were pulling away: "Don't operate, Doc, until you check that knee one more time."

So on the way to the airport, I said to the doctor: "I wish this had been like my old injury. Then you wouldn't have to operate."

That statement may have saved my career. The doctor looked at me, puzzled. "What old injury?" he asked. "During the precamp physicals, you said you'd never had a knee injury."

I almost made a bad mistake. I'd had similar injuries at Louisville, back when they gave me the shots, but the most it had ever cost me was a practice or two. The knee always tightened up again but was soon fine. I just didn't think it was worth mentioning when I went through the physical. I wasn't really trying to hide it. It had never kept me out of a game, so I didn't think of it.

The doctor started asking me questions. Apparently he believed the injury might be a chronic thing and not a new injury. We flew to Denver, but they didn't cut the knee open. They did an arthroscope, which was a new procedure then. And they gave my knee a complete examination and decided there was just some movement in my knee from the old injury. They told me I could go back to camp. Talk about your life turning around. When I got back to camp with a bandage on my knee instead of a cast, the players and the coaches couldn't believe it. They had thought I was a goner. I had a new life. My career was going to last a little longer.

But that was just the beginning. I was scared to death. I had missed a week because of the knee, and I was behind. They put me at strongside linebacker, which wasn't my natural position. In my first exhibition game we played against the Washington Redskins, and I wasn't supposed to play much because I was behind a veteran, Chip Myrtle. In the first two minutes of the game, Charlie Taylor put a crack-back block on Myrtle, and his career was over. Just like that. One block, and he's gone. That's scary.

As a trivia question, when I meet people, I ask them whom I replaced. I've never met anybody who remembers. That's sad. Chip Myrtle was a good ball player. Remember him now.

So I'm thrown into the ball game, and Joe Collier, the defensive coordinator, grabs me and says: "Whatever you do, don't let them get around your end. Watch your flank." They hand the ball off on the first play to Duane Thomas, who had just been traded to the 'Skins. I miss him on a diving tackle. He promptly goes 69 yards around my end, down to the one-yard line.

That night on the plane ride home I told Haven Moses: "They're going to cut me tomorrow morning." After that first play, Coach Collier and the other defensive coaches never said another word to me. I knew it was over. I went around shaking hands and telling the players how much I had enjoyed meeting them. I told one of the veterans I'd be watching the Broncos on television and pulling for them. "Maybe I'll see you around. Good luck," I told Haven. He finally stopped me in mid-sentence and said: "You're so foolish. Don't worry about it. Every rook goes through it." Alzado hollered at me: "You're the best linebacker who's ever played here." Suddenly that meant something, even though Lyle hadn't been around but a year. How did he know?

I didn't understand that my skills were good. I was just lacking experience. Rookies come into the league and think they have learned everything in college. And then they see somebody like Duane Thomas put a move on them they've never seen or even heard of. It's a rude awakening. You've still got so much to learn. I thought every time you gave up a first down you were going to get smacked by a coach or get cut.

What I also didn't know was that the Broncos were hurting at linebacker. This wasn't a powerhouse line-backing corps. After all, I won the starting job. And that's when I relaxed and figured out I wasn't going to get cut. I was psyched up for that home opener against Cincinnati in 1973.

Four minutes into the game I'm out for eight weeks.

I can count the plays. Nine. What a debut. I got beat on a pass pattern by a guy named Essex Johnson. I tried to hold him to keep him from getting the touchdown, and he pulled my shoulder out of place. I felt the shoulder pop out, then pop back in. But it was hurt. See ya, rookie.

The dislocation became a recurring injury, and even when I came back for the last five games of the year I had to strap down the shoulder. When you're hurt, you try to figure out ways to overcome the injury. So I developed the halo spinner technique. I could only hit someone with my left shoulder. So I worked on hitting with the left and spinning off inside to make the tackle with the same arm. What I found out after the arm healed was that the technique worked even better when one of your arms wasn't strapped down. I continued to use it, and I guess it's my most famous move. When I'm old, young linebackers will be coming to me asking about the halo spinner. It's great on the pass rush. The guard is coming at me exerting so much force. If I give him that left arm and then spin inside, I usually find myself free, and the guard is flying past me.

That year the Broncos had their first winning record, 7–5–2, and we even had a chance at the playoffs in the final game at Oakland. But that's when Ralston used that goofy fake punt on fourth down. We were at midfield and had fourth-and-10, and we were behind 14–10. That play killed us. We were stopped, and the Raiders scored three plays later and won. They took the division title. Again.

I had had a terrible year because of the shoulder. And I was beginning to wonder if the critics were right. Maybe I *was* too small, and maybe I'd stay hurt all the time. I took such a beating. For two straight days after the season I vomited. I even thought about quitting.

Later on, though, I met with Joe Collier, and he told me my play at zip linebacker in that game against Oakland was the best he'd ever seen in his career. So I figured, if I could do that with only one good shoulder, maybe I could play this game after all.

"Tommy and I are two totally different people, totally different players with totally different backgrounds. But we're like brothers. I never felt closer to another player. He would get so involved in a game. He would be screaming at the referee and the other team's players, and I would be calling our defense for the next play, and we'd line up, and Tom would walk over and ask me what the defense was. He had no idea. It didn't matter, though. He'd figure out a way to make the play.

"We actually became friends in the hospital. After my rookie year we both had to go in for surgery, so they put us in the same room. We came out of surgery in terrible pain, but we were both hungry. So we had a pizza delivered to the hospital room.

"He can get mad. Once, after practice, while Tommy was in the shower, I put some stuff called 'Atomic Balm' in his shorts. When he put them on, he nearly died. That hot balm was killing him. He ran through all the players and jumped in the ice tank. I don't think he has ever forgiven me, but he should. I made him an All-Pro."

Randy Gradishar,
Former Broncos linebacker

6
THE SPINE-TINGLING TALE OF THE BIRTH OF THE FOUR HORSEMEN AND OTHER EQUALLY EXCITING EVENTS

We still had miles to go before we could sleep, but in 1974 the Denver Broncos started to become a legitimate defense.

Several key things happened. I was moved to the weakside backer, and we switched to a three-four defense, three defensive linemen, four linebackers. We were among the first, along with the Miami Dolphins, to get out of the four-three. The idea was to take advantage of the speed and skill we had at linebacker. But that defense won't work unless you've got someone in the middle who is superior to everyone else. We had a good middle linebacker in Tom Graham, but Randolph Charles Gradishar's arrival in Denver as a rookie in 1974 made all the difference in the world. He was the highly touted number one draft pick in 1974, All-American from Ohio State.

Our initial meeting wasn't so gracious. That was the year that the NFL veterans decided to hold out and boycott the preseason games. The rookies reported. So when the rookies and free agents played an exhibition game at Mile High Stadium, I was standing outside as Randy arrived. I fired a squirt gun at him and yelled: "You scab!" He looked at me like I was a fool. Which I was.

But our relationship improved when the brief strike ended. I could tell right away Randy was a player. There had been some question about him because he had a knee injury in college, and that's why he wasn't drafted in the first two or three picks. But that knee never was a problem.

I understood Randy. I knew he had played for a great high school program in Ohio, and he was All-Everything under Woody Hayes. Plus, he was right out of the TV show "Happy Days" when I first met him: Richie Cunningham comes to the National Football League. His dad owned the grocery store in Champion, Ohio, a typical small town in the Midwest. He told me the most exciting thing that ever happened was that someone once came in and robbed the store.

We were worlds apart, a black guy from Cleveland, and a white kid from the wilds. But I don't think two guys could get any closer. I guess I could have been jealous because he was a number one pick and had played at Ohio State, but by then I had pretty much figured out that I could play the game, and that's what was important to me. I knew Randy would help our defense immensely. We were improving. Billy Thompson was a hell of a safety. Barney Chavous had been named Defensive Rookie of the Year and was something special. And we had Lyle Alzado.

We went 7–6–1 that year because we scored a lot of points. We didn't make the playoffs. The Broncos had never been to the playoffs. But we came close. We almost had a chance to be a wild card team before losing to Baltimore. We did finish just above the .500 mark.

Before the final game of the season against San

Diego, Broncos' owner Gerald Phipps came into the locker room and announced that John Ralston had been given a new, five-year contract. It was the quietest I've ever heard a locker room. Floyd Little was the only one who clapped. I heard somebody whisper: "Another five years of this shit. I want out of here." Two players did ask to be traded. I wasn't that frustrated yet, but I would be eventually. We were just beginning to jell as a team, and we had a head coach who should have been a general manager or a public realtions guy or a man who gets a bill passed to expand a stadium. He was not the guy who could coach you to the championship. He didn't know anything about the game. Guys were saying: "I can't believe they would give this yo-yo another contract." We couldn't understand why the ownership didn't know what we knew, that Ralston couldn't coach. I came of age a little bit then. I was seeing that maybe the game was about things that had nothing to do with winning, that owners were more interested in the buddy system, having a coach they felt comfortable with and who would make money for them.

We were depressed. We got destroyed by San Diego that day. Worst game we played all year. They shut us out. We didn't go out to lose the game intentionally, but our hearts weren't there. That's the closest thing I've ever seen to a game in which nobody tried to win. Gerald Phipps must have thought that his announcement would fire us up. He had no idea, no feel for what his football team was thinking. If he had come around more often, he would have known. Absentee ownership is terrible. When you own a team in this league, you need to be involved. You'd think that a guy who has made $100 million in some other business would have a clue. But most of them don't. That's why they go on giving the John Ralstons of the world contract extensions or hiring coaches who have failed miserably in other places.

After that season, though, I did have a good feeling

about myself. I hadn't been hurt, and I got some valuable experience. I had moved permanently to Denver, and even though there weren't many blacks in the city, I always felt accepted. Everything, including the football team, seemed on the way up. The energy boom was starting. Downtown Denver was exploding in growth, and the whole town seemed alive. It was a good place to be if you were young and restless.

However, in 1975 we fell back to a 6–8 record. Our offense, which had been holding us up, started to deteriorate, and the defense wasn't ready to take over yet. They were grooming Steve Ramsey to take over for Charley Johnson, and Ramsey wasn't an NFL quarterback. No way, nohow. The Raiders beat up on us the first time, something like 42–17, but I think we might have found something when we played again, this time in Oakland. We lost 17–10, but we kept it close. We started to believe.

The following year, 1976, was critical. We went 9–5, best record in the club's history, but we still didn't make the playoffs. As Otis Armstrong said: "We could have mailed in our scores and been 9–5. We should have won at least two more games." We go to Houston in the fifth game of the season with a chance to lead the division, and Max Coley, our offensive coordinator, gets sick the night before. John Ralston doesn't even know what the game plan is. Can you believe it? The head coach has no idea. Steve Ramsey had taken over as QB, and *he* had to coach the offense. What kind of confidence can you have in your head coach when you find out he doesn't know the game plan? Of course we got beat, 17–3. It's a wonder we scored any points. I think we had no first downs and about two yards of offense in the first half. Still, we had a chance to be in the playoffs until the game in New England toward the end of the season. We go charging into Boston and get drummed out 38–14. I think that was the last straw for a lot of players. As Billy

Thompson said, we had a ballet offense—one-two-three, kick.

On the brighter side, we finally had the four line-backers together. The four horsemen, they called us, from the old Notre Dame four horsemen, except that they were offensive players. The linebackers were Randy, Joe Rizzo, Bob Swenson, and I. We got so we thought as one. When one of us got cut, the other three bled. We always looked at our linebacking unit as a machine. The brain was Gradishar; the brawn was Swenson. Rizzo was our attitude, and then there was me, a ball of enthusiasm. We were four completely different guys, but we worked well together. We thought we could win a game by ourselves. We didn't care what the offense did. Put the other team on the field, and we'll score. We wanted to be on the field. We wanted to try something odd. And more times than not, we *did* make something happen. All we had to do was nod to one another. That's all it took, and we knew what to do. Joe knew everybody's assignment. Swenson didn't know anybody's assignment, but he was such a great athlete. He made more big plays than anybody, and Randy was a rock. Me, I just ran around and blitzed and kept everyone on his toes. It's not often you get four guys together in a unit who are young and can grow together. All I heard about at the Super Bowl was how good the Giants' linebacking corps was. In our day we matched them. I guarantee you.

I remember telling a reporter that year, "Some teams are afraid to show their emotions. They think it's uncool to feel that excited about a football game. I'm a hyper person, and sometimes it looks like I'm out of control. But I'm not. The linebackers are the heart of the defense, and it's our job to do the extra things to get the team psyched up."

That summed it all up. We were cruising, having a lot of fun. But we made a lot of mistakes, too. Once, against

Buffalo, we were getting killed, and on one play, a Buffalo running back got wide open. After that play, Randy and I got into an argument over who was supposed to cover that man. He maintained I should've had him, and I said he was crazy. Billy Thompson told us to shut up and play football or get off the field. But neither one of us would take him on the next play, and he gets open again and makes a touchdown.

In the locker room afterward we were still arguing about it, and Joe Collier came up and asked: "Tom, why didn't you cover that man?"

"Coach, it was Randy's man."

"No, Tom."

Randy was trying to keep from laughing.

On a point of principle I had given up a touchdown.

But playing linebacker is an incredible experience. You can block, tackle the ball carrier, get back in the pass patterns and knock down a pass or intercept it, and, of course, you can blitz the quarterback and sack him or force him to hurry his throw. It's the complete position on defense. Like a baseball catcher, you're involved in every play.

The quarterback may get the girl, but linebackers, like blondes, have more fun.

EX LIBRIS
PEGASUS

"Pound for pound, I wouldn't trade Tom Jackson for any linebacker in the league. He's the best linebacker we've ever had in Denver."

John Ralston,
Denver Broncos coach, 1974

7
MUTINY ON THE BRONCOS

The famous Denver Broncos insurrection began innocently enough when Billy Thompson called after the 1976 season ended. All he said was, "We've got to get Ralston out of here.

"Let's call up some of the guys and meet somewhere and talk about it." This was strange stuff. I'd never heard of players getting rid of their coach, except maybe the parents dumping a coach in the Pop Warner League.

It turned out that 12 veterans showed up at the Holiday Inn on Colorado Boulevard in midtown Denver, and, of course, we became known as the Dirty Dozen. This was Captain Bligh mutiny kind of talk. I felt like Mr. Christian. Will I be stranded on an island somewhere? All the players who showed up lived in Denver during the off-season—Billy, me, Tommy Lyons (who was studying to be a doctor), Bill van Heusen, Jon Keyworth, Haven Moses, Rick Upchurch, Alzado, even Otis Armstrong. Veterans who had a real stake in what

happened. Otis normally didn't do a lot of public complaining, but he was there. It was a well-rounded
bunch, about half and half from the offense and the
defense. Billy sort of became our unofficial leader, and
we talked about what we could do to oust Ralston. We
also discussed the negatives. If they didn't fire Ralston,
he would most definitely get rid of all of us. But
everybody was for it, anyway. Lyle was screaming and
hollering and throwing things. I expressed the feeling
that Ralston preached positive thinking and how it
would win football games, but that the team with the
better coach won the game. And we were working
under a handicap because of Ralston. He'd come into
one of our defensive meetings and wouldn't even know
what kind of zone we were using. We had to stop the
meeting while an assistant coach explained it to him.
We had no faith in the guy. Some of the players had
even gone to Ralston right after the 1975 season and
told him Steve Ramsey was no quarterback, and John
agreed. He said he would get another quarterback, but
he didn't. And then he came out in the papers and said
he was completely behind Ramsey and knew he could
lead us to the Super Bowl. That was taking positive
thinking much too far.

The Dirty Dozen drafted a letter that we intended to
give to owner Gerald Phipps. It said something like, "We
don't believe it is possible to win a championship under
the guidance of John Ralston. He has lost the respect of
his players, and we don't believe he is capable of
coaching us to a championship." Harsh words, but
true. By now just about everybody in town knew what
we were doing—everybody but John Ralston. He was
off scouting the Blue-Gray All-Star game with some
assistants. That night we started calling around and
found 32 veterans, out of about 45, who agreed to sign
the letter. We called a press conference for the next
morning at the hotel.

By that time, Gehrke had heard about the press

conference on the radio. He called us and said not to do anything foolish, that he and Mr. Phipps wanted to talk to us first. So they came over to the Holiday Inn and said they wanted to study the matter and make a decision without being too hasty. They asked us if we could be just a little bit patient. So we made a second draft of the letter, saying that we were totally behind the efforts of the club to do what was right, a bunch of mishmash, really. But we had to come out with something because of all the publicity we generated. Of course, the first letter got out to the press anyhow. Billy Van, a wide receiver and punter, gave just about everybody a copy, and other copies were handed out because some of the players were still really pissed. As soon as the letter got out, we heard that Mr. Phipps was furious with the players and wasn't going to do a damn thing about Ralston, because he didn't want anybody to think that the players had forced him to make a change. Nobody wanted the world to think the inmates were running the Broncos' asylum.

Management banded together. Ralston flew back and told the press: "Young people are impetuous and make mistakes. I'm not a vindictive person."

I knew we had screwed up by then. I was sure I'd be gone. Van Heusen was told by Gehrke to meet with Ralston, and he apologized all over the place and claimed he had nothing to do with it. Billy told us later there was no way Ralston was gone. I went off for Christmas and got ready for the explosion. Where would they send me? Detroit? Buffalo? I didn't even want to go to Cleveland. Billy and I went to a Denver Nuggets game, and I looked over at him and said: "We screwed up."

Then, about five weeks later, Gehrke announced that Ralston had resigned as coach. They really fired him, but it didn't matter. We had won. It didn't feel so good, but it was the right thing to do. If there hadn't been a drastic change, if Ralston had stayed, I firmly believe we never would have gone to the Super Bowl the first time.

The Broncos hired Red Miller. I didn't know much about him, except that we were going from a man who knew nothing about Xs and Os to one who knew everything about Xs and Os. Red was an assistant on that New England team that killed us and kept us out of the playoffs in 1976, and it was his game plan, we were told. The idea was, if you can't beat him, get him to join you. The other thing that happened was that we got a new quarterback, Craig Morton. I just assumed that the New York Giants didn't want to cut him, so they traded him to us for Ramsey. Craig looked like he could barely walk the last time I had seen him play. He surprised us, though. He had a lot of heart and a lot of courage.

Looking back, though, the quarterback situation might have been different if Charley Johnson had known Ralston was going. Charley hated John. If Charley had stayed, we wouldn't have acquired Craig. And I wonder if Charley would have taken us to the Super Bowl.

Nevertheless, the pressure was on the veterans. We now had to go out and prove we were a championship ball club, that the only thing holding us back was the coach. Red Miller was slightly surprised that the team didn't have any discipline problems, despite the mutiny. He expected to have to lie down with lions, and instead he got a bunch of pussycats. We didn't need problems. We needed to win.

Because if we didn't, Ralston would have the last laugh.

"I always thought Tom Jackson was a great player. A real emotional guy. But I don't think he ever liked me. He came over to the sidelines once when the Broncos were beating us and screamed: 'It's all over, fat man.' He still doesn't like me. The only reason he talked to me before one game last season was because he had the flu and he wanted to give it to me."

John Madden,
Ex-Raiders coach

8
CAN THE DENVER BRONCOS FORGET JOHN RALSTON AND FIND TRUE HAPPINESS IN THE SUPER BOWL?

EX LIBRIS
PEGASUS

It was a day for suckin' air and dyin'. That was the first day in training camp in 1977, the first of the two-a-day practices, the first day of a whole new era, the first day of the rest of my life. We had a new coach, a new quarterback, a new attitude. And it felt good.

I was so certain that 1977 would be our year that I went around bragging to the media. Probably shouldn't have been shooting my mouth off, and some people in the NFL thought I was just being a court jester again. But I had a feeling. I said we would win 11 games. Guaranteed it. Of course I was wrong. We didn't win 11. We won 12. My mouth almost got me in trouble, though. I told Joe Sanchez of *The Denver Post* in training camp that Randy Gradishar was 10 times the linebacker that Jack Lambert was and that we were going to beat Oakland "and then we're gonna keep beating 'em and beating 'em." I said, "We're gonna win a lot of football games this year. The way I see it, we're going to win the first 4, 2 of the next 4, and 5 of the last

6. Hey, we should have won 11 last year, and we're a better team." Well, we did win our first 4. In fact, we won our first 6 before losing one, and then we didn't lose again until the last game. I got carried away a little, saying that we were going to stuff people and kick the Raiders. But we backed it up.

Right away we knew there was something special about 1977 when we beat the St. Louis Cardinals 7–0 in the opener. They had the most high-powered offense in the league—Don Coryell was their coach then—and they got nothing off us. Our defense was just so tremendously confident as the weeks went on. We had four or five ball players who were the best in the league at their position, guys like Louis Wright and Billy Thompson, Gradishar, Alzado, me. We didn't care what the offense did. If they threw a couple of interceptions or laid it down three or four times, it didn't matter. If we got behind, the defense just said, "That's OK, we'll score." We'd intercept the pass and lateral the football three or four times. We were almost like the Harlem Globetrotters. When you've got great defense, you're never out of a game.

In our second game of the 1977 season we played Buffalo and the fabled O.J., and suddenly, our linebacking corps was being talked about outside our camp. Kay Dalton, who was an assistant with Buffalo, told a writer that "those four Denver linebackers are about as talented a bunch as anywhere in football." Some respect. And that's when a writer came up with the Orange Crush nickname. It fit, and it stuck.

We held O.J. to less than 50 yards and beat Buffalo, and I was beginning to feel like we had it going.

That was a game in which I pulled off one of my best all-time tricks. The Bills were getting ready to try a 52-yard field goal, and I hollered out: "Hey, ref, they got 12 men on the field." The Bills' holder stopped and counted their players. And the 30-second clock ran out on them. It pushed them back 5 yards and out of field goal range.

Of course, they only had 11 players on the field. But you do what you can in the heat of battle. I always like to mess with their minds. I love to play chess, and football has some of the same characteristics. You've got to figure two and three steps ahead and plan an attack. I may look like I'm limping, so they'll run or throw my way. I may not blitz for three quarters, saving it for the play when we most need it.

The next two games we beat Seattle and Kansas City, and I got my first interception of the year against the Chiefs, setting up a touchdown. I ended up with six interceptions in '77 to go with the seven in '76. Thirteen in two years. No other linebacker was close.

But then came the big one against the Oakland Raiders. A writer asked me that week to describe the game:

"Mojo go to Oakland, walk on hot coals." I don't know what it meant, but it sounded tough.

This was the first time that both the Raiders and the Broncos came into a game undefeated. Ken Stabler sort of surprised us that day. He came out throwing. Normally they would try to run the ball down our throats. Their game plan was perfect for us. We couldn't match their strength, but we could stop them in the air. Our linebacker coach, Myrel Moore, called us together on the sidelines and told us to jump all over their tight end, Dave Casper, and their running backs. Just beat the hell out of them. Joe Rizzo picked off a pass, and we scored, and then he got another interception, and I knew we had them. If Joe is picking off passes, Oakland is in deep trouble. We were up 21–7 at halftime. Then it got better. Billy Thompson intercepted two passes. Rizzo got another one, and even Paul Smith got a pick. We intercepted Stabler a record seven times. And I got a fumble that led to the most memorable moment in my career. I picked up the ball, waved it around, and then looked up at the Oakland coach, John Madden, and said: "It's all over, fat man."

The king was dead. The reign was over. We beat the Raiders.

Stabler had played his worst pro game. I'll never forget Stabler saying after the game, "They just beat the crap out of us. Maybe you will believe me when I say this is a tough division."

I began shouting in the locker room, "We beat the world champions. We're better than the world champions." We floated home on beer, and there must have been 10,000 people at the airport. As we walked through the airport everyone slapped us on the back and shouted encouragement and spilled beer on us. It was an incredible celebration. The players had never experienced anything like that. That was the first time in the history of the Denver Broncos that we had won a big road game and come home to find a reception like that. It was a sign of things to come.

And it was time for Oakland again. Now this game was even bigger. In Denver, nationally televised, suddenly we're being noticed by the national media. It took me a few days to get over my leg problems, but no way was I going to miss this one. Particularly after we read that Monte Johnson of the Raiders said after the first game: "They beat us today, but we're the better team. If we play them 10 times, we'll win the next 9."

Well, they did win. They had gotten smarter since the first game. They didn't throw the ball. They ran and ran, and we weren't as effective. I remember someone asking Myrel Moore on the sidelines how we were going to stop the Raiders' running game. "Get me a shotgun, and I'll stop it," he said. That's what it would have taken that day.

We were still 6–1, but you wouldn't believe it from the national media. They were calling us orange pumpkins. Everybody thought we were just a fluke. The Raiders were back. Forget Denver. Go crawl in your hole, Broncos. So we still had to prove a thing or two.

We won against Pittsburgh and then against San

Diego (despite my mistake, which I'll get to later) and then went over to Kansas City, where we won again by killing an important drive.

That's the way the season was going for us. For years we had buzzards' luck. We couldn't kill anything, and we couldn't get anything to die. But in 1977 we had all the luck. If we had gone to Las Vegas and put one dime in the slot machine, we'd have won a million bucks. We felt like a million bucks.

"Hey, nigger," the fan letter began. That piqued my attention. So I read on.

"The next time you intercept a pass, stick the ball up your ass. Maybe you won't fumble it that way."

My pen pal didn't care for what I did in the game at San Diego.

We were leading 17–14. With time running out I intercepted a pass and was coasting down the sidelines for a sure touchdown when I dropped the ball. Just dropped it. Nobody touched me. I didn't trip. I just dropped the ball. Occasionally you're just stupid. This was my occasion.

San Diego got the ball back and had a chance to tie the game, but not much of a chance. I told the linebackers they'd better not let San Diego score, or my ass would be natural grass. I didn't want to be remembered as one of those guys who pick up a fumble and run it the length of the field the wrong way. So we won, but there was still a bunch of unhappy people, I found out the next day. Apparently, the betting line was four points on that game. If I had run that interception back for a touchdown, we would have covered the spread. But I fumbled the ball. So I got a letter. Or two. Somebody told me that fumble may have cost bettors a million dollars. I guess my pen pal was in that group.

A couple of weeks later in Mile High Stadium we had a chance to beat Baltimore and be in the playoffs for the first time. I loved to play against Bert Jones, their quarterback. Until John Elway came along, Jones threw the hardest pass in the league, and he was a real challenge to play against. On this particular play Baltimore had a quick back against a linebacker, and when you've got an arm like Jones, the pass is almost a cinch. They ran this play during the game four times. Four exactly. The first time they ran the play it was incomplete. The second time Bert tried it the pass was complete, and I made a dive for the ball and barely touched it. The next time Bert threw it on third down neither one of us could get to it.

Fourth quarter, we're ahead 20–13, Baltimore has the ball in our territory, and Bert Jones is driving the Colts for the tying touchdown. Suddenly, I know exactly what play they're going to run, and everything clicks in for me. I said to myself, He's getting ready to run this route, and it's a crucial situation, and Bert's been depending on that play. And here's your big chance, Tom. Intercept the pass and run it for the touchdown, and be the big hero. It's amazing what you can say to yourself at a time like that. You forget the crowd and everything else. It's just me and Bert.

I immediately made a break toward the line of scrimmage. Now, if you break toward the ball on that play and miss it, there's nobody behind you to make the tackle, and it's TD. So many guys in this league are afraid of looking like fools. They're afraid of being aggressive. They make the safe play, and the other team gets the first down. But that's not the way the game's supposed to be played. You go for it. If I get there, I'll knock it down or intercept the ball. If I don't get there, he's gone. History. I felt confident. Bert threw it eyehigh, and about the time he let it go he saw me. I saw his eyes, and he knew.

He knew I had the ball. For a moment I could see the fear.

I picked off the pass, and my only thought was: just run. I never looked back. It was absolutely silent. Sure, 75,000 people are screaming, and the players on both sides are yelling, but you don't hear a thing. You don't feel anything. It's slow motion. My mind focused on one thing. I could see the end of the field, and I just wanted to get there.

After I ran about 30 yards, I turned to see if Bert was there because he was the only one who had a chance to get me. But he wasn't anywhere around. I hit that end zone, and my whole body relaxed. It's like an orgasm. Your body just sinks and quits. There's this tremendous roar, and I threw the ball into the stands. And as soon as I let go of the ball I remembered that the league fines you if you throw away a football. So let 'em fine me. There was a mob in the end zone. I think the whole stadium was on top of me, and the players carried me off the field. I didn't know until later it was the longest interception return in the team's history.

Oh, I did have one other thought as I was running down the field:

Whatever you do, Tom, don't drop this football like you did in San Diego. You'll get another letter from that asshole who called you a nigger. So I tucked that ball away, and we won the game 27–13, and if you're somewhere out there reading this, pen pal, you can stick that right up your ass.

I didn't realize the implications of that play at the time, but it turned out to be the biggest play of the year for me and the team. Because we beat Baltimore we ended up getting the home field advantage in the playoffs, and we went on to the Super Bowl.

Playoffs, Pittsburgh, Christmas Eve. I got the first indication it was my day when Franco Harris was smacked by Lyle Alzado early in the second quarter, fumbled, and I picked it up and ran to the 10, and Otis Armstrong scored on the next play to give us a 14–0 lead. Then, right before the half, 14–14, Mean Joe Greene got into it with a couple of our players. He sucker-punched Paul Howard and then hit Mike Montler later. Red Miller was on a tear. He wanted to take Greene on himself. Instead, as the half ended, Red went after their defensive coordinator, George Perles. We had to pull them apart, but we loved it. You couldn't just beat Pittsburgh. You had to knock them out.

In the fourth quarter, we kicked a field goal and were clinging to a 24–21 lead with about seven minutes to go. I knew Terry Bradshaw had to pass. And I was waiting. At the Pittsburgh 40 I jumped up as high as I could go, barely tipped the ball with my left hand, and got ahold of it with my right. I ran to the 9-yard line before they stopped me. I still have a picture someone took of me running down the sidelines. I had a smile that reached out of my helmet.

We managed only a field goal, though, so a Pittsburgh TD would win it. Bradshaw wasn't gun-shy. He came back throwing. I was waiting again. I intercepted his pass at the 50 and ran it down to the 33. Two interceptions and a fumble recovery. Not in my wildest dreams.

OK, offense. It's up to you. Don't blow it again. Craig Morton went up top and hit Haven Moses, the M&M Connection, for a touchdown, and it was all over. My three turnovers led directly to 17 points. Somebody wrote in the paper that I was a black Santa Claus. What more could you ask for? It was the game for which I'd brought my father out to Denver, and he was waiting outside in the darkness under the stadium for me. I signed a hundred autographs or more, and my father was off to the side. Finally, we got away and jumped in the car. He told me I played a pretty good game. I think every son can appreciate it when his father really is proud of him. God, I felt good. That meant more to me than making All-Pro or being voted Best Defensive Player or even winning the playoff game. If only Mom had been there to share it with us, I could have quit the game right there.

We played Oakland for the AFC championship. It was only fitting.

New Year's Day, 1978. Our major concern was the health of Craig Morton. He had an extremely bad bruise on his hip—the whole side of his leg and his butt were purple and black and blue and red, and he had been in the hospital all week. It was supposed to be a secret, and we didn't even know if he could play until the warm-ups. Meanwhile, the Raiders came to town acting like their usual asshole selves, wearing their Super Bowl rings and talking about how they would beat us bad. "After we beat the Broncos," linebacker Floyd Rice said, "I'm going to get a can of orange pop, open it and turn it upside down, and pour it out . . . slowly."

In the locker room Craig was still so pained that, when Red Miller went over to ask him if he could play, Craig told him he couldn't even tie his shoes. So there was our coach, tying the quarterback's shoes.

But Craig hung in there. If he had been sacked, I think he would have been finished. But the offensive linemen were aware of how hurt he was, and they played their best game. At the half we were up 7–3. Red wrote on the blackboard in the locker room, "30 Minutes to the Super Bowl." He didn't say a thing.

The Raiders weren't doing anything against our defense, but our offense wasn't burning a hole in them, either. We moved to the two-yard line, where the famous no-fumble play occurred. This was long before they started using instant replays, but this might have been the play that made them start thinking about it. Our running back, Rob Lytle, went up in the air at the two, was hit, and dropped the ball, but the ref ruled there was no fumble. I think everyone admits now that Lytle really did fumble, but after all the breaks the Raiders got over the years and after all their cheating, it was only fair. In fact, it was perfect. Die by the sword, you Raiders. It was their turn to suffer.

On the next play we got the touchdown and had a 14–3 lead.

Right after that, Joe Rizzo put a vicious hit on Fred Biletnikoff, breaking his collarbone. And without their best receiver, the Raiders were in deep trouble. We would have been ahead by even more, but Jim Turner missed his third field goal. Everyone remembers that Rich Karlis missed those field goals in the Super Bowl against the Giants because we lost, but everyone has conveniently forgotten that Jim Turner, the great talk show host, missed three in the AFC championship game. They forgot because we won the game, 20–17.

The place went mad. I've never witnessed anything like it. Haven was doing cartwheels up and down the field. All 75,000 fans poured onto the field. It was like the world was coming to an end. Maybe it was. We had finally beaten the Raiders for the championship. Both goalposts were torn down, and fans took pieces of turf and pieces of our uniforms as souvenirs. I was jumping and hollering with Billy Thompson. One of the Raiders, Mark van Eeghen, I think, came over and took my hand and said: "Go get the ring now." And everyone was chanting over and over: "Super Bowl."

"I wonder where John Ralston is now," Billy Thompson said to me.

"I don't know where he is. But I'm in heaven," I said.

"Let's go to New Orleans!" I screamed at the south stands. The Battle of New Orleans. Denver in the Super Bowl. It sure felt good. And I remembered that Dallas's big mouth linebacker, Tom "Hollywood" Henderson, said after we lost to them in the final regular-season game that "If this is a Super Bowl preview, I'm going out now and buying a house, because we're going to get the winner's share, for sure." I wanted to make him eat those words.

This was it. The pinnacle of success in pro football. We had a fantastic send-off in Denver, rode an orange Braniff plane to New Orleans, and were greeted by several hundred Broncomaniacs who were already in Louisiana a week early. Or maybe we had more fans around the country than I realized. Finally, we were getting some respect.

A rude awakening. The buses took us to this terrible motel. All those years of playing football and hearing about the Super Bowl, and my bed has roaches in it, and the paint is peeling off the walls in the room, and they can't even make a decent sandwich in the motel restaurant. We spent the whole week going across the street to eat at McDonald's. Welcome to the Super Bowl. The players were incensed. Otis Armstrong brought one of the roaches to practice, gave it a name, and called it the team mascot. A bunch of players got stuck in the hotel elevator, and we were beginning to think we might not even make it to the Super Bowl. "32 Broncos Eaten by Roaches, Rest Lost in Elevator," the headline would say.

There was one big difference between that Super Bowl and the one in Pasadena. Everything in California is so spread out. In New Orleans everybody was in the French Quarter or at the two or three hotels, and I had a feeling all week that a party was going on. I never got that impression in California.

Most of us played it low-key in New Orleans. I remember the second night, the linebackers went out to dinner together and got it out of our systems, but otherwise we stayed out of the way. Glenn Hyde, a backup offensive lineman, hung out in the French Quarter all week and did enough celebrating for the rest of us. The one night we did go to dinner, we strolled down Bourbon Street to get a cab, and a bar owner recognized us. He invited us in, gave us Super Bowl T-shirts and drinks all around, and slobbered all over us. We felt like real big shots. Until we got ready to leave and he handed us a bill for $60, for the shirts and the drinks. We gave the T-shirts back.

The Cowboys worked out at the Saints' field, while we got stuck at the old Sugar Bowl at Tulane Stadium. It had been abandoned and looked like it. It was as if it had been hit by a bomb. The artificial turf was ripped up in several places. Wide receivers would go out on pass routes and trip on the rug. And the dressing rooms were awful. They stank. All week long the weather was terrible, too. Cold and overcast. I was expecting something better.

But our defense was gaining some recognition. At the press conferences, writers were talking to us about the Orange Crush and how the four linebackers had come together, and we decided to forget all the other trash and just go out and beat the powerful Cowboys.

I woke up that morning believing I would go to bed a world champion that night. But I didn't understand what was going on in Craig Morton's mind. Dallas had really messed up his brain over the years. I guess he never got over the way the Cowboys had treated him during the peak years of his career. He just wasn't himself. Besides, he and everyone else knew the Cowboys would be coming after him. That was their game plan. Get Craig. Cliff Harris said: "Craig will never finish the game." He was right. Craig was useless. He felt we didn't have a chance because Tom Glassic weighed only 219 pounds. Glassic, our left guard, had been suffering with a bad throat. When he weighed in during Super Bowl week Tom was way down from 235–240. He looked skinny. Craig saw it and became real frightened thinking about Randy White, all 270 pounds, against a guy who weighed 50 pounds less. Craig knew White would be in his face all day. Well, if the quarterback thinks we're beat, what chance do we have? I never forgave Craig for his attitude that day. We were beaten before we started.

I'll never forget those first few minutes in the Superdome. I could see all the people from Denver upstairs, dressed in orange, waving their signs. We were told that about 40,000 people had made the trip in motor homes, by car, by plane, and even by hitchhiking. It took my breath away. I really had butterflies. Despite all the bad parts of the week, the first few minutes of the Super Bowl were very special. This is what you play for.

The first time our offense got the ball, we picked up one first down, but then Randy White sacked Craig. Craig spent the rest of the half looking at Randy White. He has probably spent the rest of his life thinking about Randy White waiting to tear him limb from limb.

Things just got progressively worse. Craig threw an interception, then another, then a third. Jack Dolbin fumbled a pass reception. Riley Odoms fumbled a catch. And Craig threw still another interception. He had been intercepted only eight times all season. Craig was saving his worst for last. I guess he wanted to beat his old team so bad that he couldn't do anything right. Afterward I saw one story that said: "After all these years Craig Morton finally led the Dallas Cowboys to a Super Bowl victory." Cruel, but accurate. Our offense could do nothing right, but, fortunately, the defense had its fingers in the dike. We were trying to hold off the flood.

At halftime, lucky to be behind only 13–0, Red wrote on the blackboard: "7 turnovers, 13 points, tuck the ball away, hit hard, defense, 30 minutes, settle down." The offense certainly had to settle down if we were to have any chance. But it took only one look around the locker room to understand what was going to happen in the second half. We've got a defense chanting about how we're going to kill their ass, and the offensive players are sitting there, helmets and heads down, not saying a word. They believed they had lost the football game, and they had. Our defense couldn't beat the combination of Dallas and our offense.

We got a field goal early in the third quarter, so we still had a hope. Butch Johnson fumbled the kickoff but got it back at the 21. We stopped them, but Craig was sacked. At least he didn't throw another interception.

That's when Roger Staubach, on third down, hit Butch on a fly pattern for a 45-yard touchdown. It was 20–3, and we were finished, even though we still had more than a quarter to go. One of these days we're going to be in a close Super Bowl at the end. Final score, 27–10.

I'll never forget how, as we were walking off the field, our fans stood up in the end zone and sang: "We love you, Broncos." All was not lost.

I knew we had to come back to the Super Bowl and redeem ourselves. I just didn't realize it would take so long to return.

"Tom Jackson doesn't like the Raiders too much. I should say he hates the Raiders. I don't know what got into him. What was it we did? I know he's a good player, but when he plays us, he's an incredible player."

Tom Flores,
Los Angeles Raiders coach

9
MOJO AND THE RAIDERS OF THE LOST ARK: HOW I WALKED ON HOT COALS

EX LIBRIS
PEGASUS

I don't care who the players are or what city they're in. They're still the Oakland Raiders to me. I'd chase them to the end of the earth and crawl even farther just to get after them. I love the rivalry. They are skull and crossbones. They are silver and black. They're everything disgusting in a football team. They're the devils of pro football, and I hate them.

I think you get the idea. I never liked the Raiders. I can't fix my mouth to say anything good about the Raiders. They make me so mad.

They're a lot like the Chicago Bears, but their work ethic might not be as principled as the Bears'. The Raiders believe in cheating to win. Maybe they think that if you're not cheating you don't want it as bad. I've seen things. I'll reflect on one play that will stay on my mind forever. It was the game between the Raiders and the Chargers years ago, and on the final play of the game Kenny Stabler can't find anybody open, and he's getting a tremendous pass rush, and he looks as if he is fumbling the football. He fumbles it 20 yards ahead, and Pete Banaszak looks like he's trying to pick it up, but he fumbles it ahead another 10 yards or so to the 1-yard line. Dave Casper comes along, and he can't quite get a handle on it until he pushes it 3 yards deep into the end zone and falls on it. The way the Raiders got the ball into the end zone to beat the Chargers was like watching a soccer game. I am screaming at my TV and to the refs: "They're cheating. Don't let them get away with it." But they did. The Raiders always do.

The thing is, if the Raiders had said nothing, they could have kept doing it. But they got into the locker room and actually bragged about what they did to the Chargers and the refs. The NFL later changed the rule because of that play.

I would venture to say most teams couldn't be successful doing what the Raiders do. They're the most penalized team in football year after year, a stat they're proud of. But they have had great success, setting a winning tradition in intimidation and penalties.

And they love to spit on you.

But all that aside, the reason they really win is that they've had a lot of gifted athletes. Ted Hendricks and Ken Stabler, Cliff Branch and Dave Casper. Now they have Howie Long and Marcus Allen. Yeah, you can win with people like that. And they save people's careers. Lyle Alzado was dead until he landed on his feet with the Raiders. Now the man has a Hollywood career. He left Denver crying and went to Cleveland. And Cleveland wanted to get rid of him. He ended up with the Raiders, and his career was renewed because of the people around him.

My results against the Raiders are a lot better than most people's. In the games I've played against them—I missed 4 because of injury, and we lost 3 and tied 1—they've won 14, and we've won 11. Now keep in mind that from 1973 to 1976 we won only once, so since then we've each won about the same number of games. It's been a war.

I don't know how this hatred of the Raiders started, really. I didn't grow up hating the Raiders. I guess it was a result of coming to Denver and hearing all around the league about how great the Raiders were and how awful the Broncos had been for so long. Once I became established, I wanted to make sure we didn't have to listen to that crap forever. I developed a healthy respect for the Raiders, but our games with them took on a personal stake for me. Every time we played them I got so worked up, and when we beat them it was especially good. I love to go eyeball to eyeball and stick it in their eyeball. Lining up on the side with Gene Upshaw and Art Shell and knowing that the Raiders were going to run kept me determined. It also gave me a lot of pain.

What I will remember most is going to Oakland in 1977 and just kicking their butts. Jim Turner even scored on a fake field goal when he caught a pass from Norris Weese. Joe Rizzo had three interceptions, and we were all over them. They couldn't do anything right. We ended up winning 30–7, and we even let them have that one touchdown.

The play in that game I'll always be remembered for, though, is when I called John Madden "fat man." I recovered a fumble near their sideline late in the second half, and John Madden had run all the way down from their bench. He was standing right there—four feet away—looking at me when I got up. If he hadn't been there, I wouldn't have said anything. Or I might have taunted one of the Raiders, maybe said something like "You jerk, you." But at that moment I released all the frustrations of so many years and so many Broncos who had been wanting to beat the Raiders and get to the playoffs. So I said, "It's all over, fat man." What I meant was that the dominance was over. Never again would we have to be afraid of the Raiders. We were just as good as or better than they were. For so long they were the high-and-mighty because they annually thumped us. We were a gnat to them. But the reign was over. The spell was broken. They weren't going to win

19 out of 20 ever again. "It's all over, fat man." The look on his face at that moment said he agreed with me.

For a long time, if the Raiders lost to us, the comments in their locker room were: "No big deal. We'll come back and win the next four. Losing to the Broncos was nothing. They act like they won the Super Bowl." But to us, beating the Raiders was what we needed to gain some self-acceptance. We knew we could play with anybody if we could beat the Raiders. There was a game where Bill Pickel, their nose tackle, got hurt, and Matt Millen, one of their linebackers, screamed at him, "Get up, Pick, they can't hurt you. These are the Broncos. They can't hurt anybody." Two plays later Millen himself had to be helped off the field. Need I say more?

I'm proud that we won the two meetings in 1986, but it's almost kind of sad now. The relationship with the Raiders has gone full circle. We're better than they are. I don't feel sorry for them or anything, but they're not in our class anymore. The great and powerful Raiders are just an average football team now. We went from being beaten by them all the time, to splitting games, to losing to them in overtime in games that could go either way, to winning in L.A., 21–10. That's the Broncos, 21–10 on the Raiders' home field.

I like John Madden now. I hated him then because he represented what the Raiders stood for, nastiness. He was the head of the silver and black. He was the captain of the skull and crossbones ship. He was like them. He roared on the sidelines. We could hear him on the field screaming at them and screaming at us. He wasn't always just a lovable teddy bear. He intimidated the refs worse than anybody I ever saw. But he's a super commentator. I like him in the booth, but I hate the fact that he's still not there for me to point at.

The games with the Raiders will always stand out for me, like the one in 1975, when we led 17–7 with four minutes left in the third quarter, and we had the ball on their one-yard line with goal to go. We wound up losing 42–17. I remember sacking Plunkett in 1983 and causing a fumble, and Barney Chavous recovered it for a touchdown. That was a big game for me. I caused two fumbles. I also got Marcus Allen for a three-yard loss when the Raiders were on our four-yard line. But it didn't matter. They beat us in overtime, 22–20. God, we had some close games with them. I also remember the first play in overtime in 1986, when Marcus Allen started around me and got 14 yards on the play. In the 1984 overtime game Steve Watson came over to me on the sidelines and said: "Watch this. I'm going to go make a touchdown catch." And he sure as hell did. Against Lester Hayes.

I enjoyed playing against Marv Hubbard and Dave Casper and Todd Christensen and Fred Biletnikoff and Gene Upshaw and Art Shell, but the one Raider I will remember the most is Kenny Stabler. He had a calm about him that made him the most dangerous in the last two minutes of a game. I used to do an impression of him during practice the week leading up to a game. He had a unique style as a left-hander. I'd line up under center, take the ball left-handed, and do a three-step straight-legged drop, pump once—because he always pump-faked first—and look left and then look right and then look back left and, finally, throw. He looked at every possible receiver on the field. I've seen him do that 90,000 times on film and complete the pass. It was a pure form of flattery, and it was a joke when I did it. But he was no joke. You have to appreciate that Stabler was a hard liver, but that didn't matter. He was so perfect, so fundamentally sound. He'd always air the ball out, throw it deep early in the game to make us aware that he could throw long. Then when we started cheating back, he'd come underneath. When you went against him, it was the ultimate challenge, a game of strategy, a chess match.

I like Marcus Allen a lot now because he's as good a

running back as I've ever seen. I broke a long-standing
rule and went to the Raiders' locker room in 1985 and
shook his hand and told him how much I thought of his
ability. He's the kind of guy that if you hit him, he looks
at you and says: "Good tackle." Karl Mecklenburg put
the most vicious lick on Marcus Allen I've ever seen. He
caught him just right. You don't get that often. I'll tell
you the kind of guy Allen is. He got up groggy, but went
back to the huddle and asked for the ball again. He
didn't want anybody to think he couldn't take it. We
were all surprised when he got the ball on the next play.
You gain respect for a guy right away. He's one of the
few quadruple threats in football; he'll run, catch,
throw, and even throw a block. He has courage and a
big heart.

Myrel Moore told me he thought if we played the
Raiders every week, I would be the best linebacker in
the history of football. Maybe so. That's one game I
could always gear up for and play my best. You hear
players all the time talking about giving 120 percent.
The truth is you actually give 75 or 80 percent most of
the time. And that's pretty good, considering. But
against the Raiders I always gave 120 percent.

When I think of one individual with the Raiders, I
always think of Al Davis, their owner and general
manager. Every time we played them he would come
over to where we were warming up before the game,
wearing the same black leather jacket and the silver
pants. I heard he wore black and silver all the time
because he was color-blind. But he wasn't blind. He
knew what he was doing. He was trying to psyche us
out or something. He just stood there, never saying
anything. He's what the Raiders are all about. He is the
sculptor. Because of him, no matter who the players or
the coaches are, the Raiders' style never seems to
change. Throw long, run at you, try to hurt you from
the defensive side. Interestingly, the Raiders have always had lousy special teams. Maybe Al doesn't care

much about special teams play. But he's a winner. You have to admire him for that.

I've never said this publicly, but I think I could have been the best Raider of all time. Though I hate to admit it, I was perfectly suited for playing in a Raiders' uniform. But it was probably more fun to just play against them.

"Not only is Tom Jackson the biggest practical joker on the team—he once ordered six pizzas from a place and then poured water on the guy and his pizzas when he delivered them to the training camp dorm—but he should be on the Johnny Carson show with his impressions. Only he does strange impressions. He does John Ralston and Ken Stabler. He doesn't do John Wayne. If he hadn't gone into football, T.J. would have been a stand-up comedian. There have been a lot of days when I've come to practice down because of personal problems, but once you're around Tom, you forget your problems. His enthusiasm is infectious."

Jim Ryan,
Broncos linebacker

10

THE MAN WITH THE GOLDEN ARM: HOW I STOPPED WORRYING AND LEARNED TO LOVE THE BOMB

EX LIBRIS
PEGASUS

In the afterglow of Super Bowl XII, it was time to start taking care of business, my personal finances. I was supposed to get my just reward. Remember, I originally signed a contract for $21,500, then a few more bucks the other two years. I had gone back in after the 1976 season to negotiate a new contract, and they told me I hadn't become All-Pro, the Broncos hadn't won their division, and we hadn't gone to the Super Bowl. I didn't have any leverage. This time I did. I had been to the Pro Bowl. We had won our division and had been to the Big Bowl. I was one of the league's best players at my position, and I deserved to be paid like one.

That's when you discover the harsh realities. I asked the club to be fair. But fair has nothing to do with it. I asked general manager Fred Gehrke, "What do you think I deserve?" When he told me a figure, well under $100,000, it was like a slap in the face. He embarrassed me. No one loves football more than I do, and I would have played back in the old days for $100 a game. But there were linebackers making $250,000, and I thought I should get at least some of that, not just crumbs. They were only interested in paying me the lowest possible amount.

It bothered me that you work hard and accomplish all the things you're told you must do, and then that's not enough. I had come into the league unknown, and I accepted what they gave me. Then, the second time around, I again accepted what they wanted to give me because they told me I wasn't "that good" yet. But when I got "that good" they still didn't want to pay me. A little bit goes out of you then. People wonder why players aren't loyal. Maybe we'd be more loyal if the teams were a little bit loyal.

I had no option. The Broncos weren't going to trade me, they weren't going to free me, and they didn't want to pay me. They kept saying: "We don't want things to get out of hand contractually with the players." The game has always been fun for me, but I realized that for them, it was only a business.

But they couldn't make me lose my love of the sport. I didn't have as strong a feeling for the NFL as I had had in the past, but I still had a strong feeling for football.

It never has been that I wanted the money for extravagant things. Once I got that Monte Carlo with my bonus check, that pretty much took care of the flash. My idea of blowing money is to get a new pair of sweats and a chiliburger.

It's funny how some athletes are with money. Take Gradishar. Once, at Cleveland, the Browns were on our one-yard line, third down. We had stopped them twice. Right in the middle of our defensive huddle Randy stopped talking and reached down. He saw a dime lying on the ground right at the goal line. There we were, 70,000 people screaming, the biggest moment in the game, and Randy, who makes a ton of money, has found a dime. The whole defensive team was laughing when the Browns came up the line. They didn't know if we were laughing at them or what. Randy, meanwhile, is trying to figure out where to put the dime. He stuck it in his pants, made the tackle, and we stopped them again. Shows how free Randy is with his money.

Randy and I were always having wild times on the field. Randy called it "Broncoland," like it was an amusement park. Football was never the real world to him. Once against Seattle we both screwed up. He went outside when he was supposed to go over the middle, and I went inside when I was supposed to come around the outside. We both forgot the play. But the Seahawks weren't expecting it, and we both got there at the same time and made the sack. On the sideline Myrel Moore said: "I don't know what you're doing out there, and I don't think you two do, either, but whatever it is, keep on doing it."

One time Randy called, "Gap, Mike, shoot, cover one," a defense designed for him to blitz up the middle. Well, Randy got down in a three-point stance over the guard, something he had never done in all his years with the Broncos. Jim Zorn, the Seattle quarterback, told us later he didn't know what was going on. They had never seen Randy down like that before. Well, Randy saw that he couldn't get past the guard, so at the last second he dropped back and intercepted a pass. The Seahawks were so confused that they threw it right to him. I went over to him after the play and asked: "What in the hell was that?" Randy just shrugged. He didn't know either.

The NFL added two more games to the schedule in 1978, and I honestly think it affected defenses more. Scoring started going up. Defenses wore down. Teams were willing to take more chances because there were 16 games, and maybe one loss didn't mean as much.

We win the division for the second straight year with a 10–6 record and go into the playoffs in Pittsburgh feeling pretty good. After the game we don't feel so good. I think that Pittsburgh team may have been the greatest team ever. It was the best team I've ever played against, Giants and Cowboys and Raiders included.

I thought our defense was special, but I have to admit Pittsburgh's was even better. The whole Pro Bowl starting linebacker unit was made up of guys from Pittsburgh, and Randy and I were the backups. They had two or three All-Pro linemen, a Hall of Famer in Mean Joe Greene, and some great defensive backs. And bam! They ended our season rather abruptly. No Super Bowl. They kicked us 33–10 and went on to win the Super Bowl over Dallas in the best Super Bowl game ever played. If you have to go to Three Rivers Stadium at that time of the year, you have no chance. That artificial turf is frozen. It's like playing on a hockey rink. You can't put on enough padding. You might as well be playing in the parking lot.

Maybe Red Miller was a little out of control as a coach by then. There's a tendency for all successful coaches to think they're the second coming of Vince Lombardi. "I take a team that's not so talented and take them to the Bowl. I must be good." But that's not the reason we went. We had the "D." And Joe Collier certainly had a lot to do with it, and the players who had put their necks on the block to get rid of Ralston had a lot of motivation. But Red started to believe he was the sole reason we won 24 games in two seasons.

It was beginning to dawn on me that we probably wouldn't go back to the Super Bowl until we got some offense. Billy Thompson used to say to me: "Look at the teams in the Super Bowl. They have good defenses, yes, but they got weapons on offense." We had a popgun offense, and Craig was getting older and older, and we were getting more and more conservative in a liberal league.

The next year, 1979, is a blur. We get to the playoffs as a wild card and play in Houston. We knock out Earl Campbell, Dan Pastorini, and Kenny Burroughs in the first half. Even the score that Houston does get in the first half is tainted because when we look at the films the next year we see that Campbell fumbled before he got to the end zone, and the official couldn't see it. So we have a chance. We have the "D." In the second half we get a turnover on Houston's 22-yard line. Four downs later we've been backed up 34 yards and have to punt. There's no way we can win.

After that, the defense basically caved in. We knew, as long as we didn't have an offense, we were going to continue to fade. We lost, of course. The defense was getting sick and tired of playing its butt off and having an offense that couldn't do a damn thing.

The other thing that bothered me about 1979 was my first real "injury." I got an ulcer. That's right. Me, happy-go-lucky Tom Jackson. I thought ulcers were for overweight, 50-year-old stockbrokers. How could Tom Jackson get an ulcer? The doctor told me there was no rhyme or reason for ulcers. It didn't have to be because you worried. I was worried about the team falling back a couple of steps, but I didn't deserve an ulcer. The doctors finally concluded that my ulcer was the result of too many middle-of-the-night trips to Pizza Hut and the House of Pies. They gave me some medication and a bottle of Maalox and told me to start watching my diet. And I did. I stayed away from hamburgers for about a week.

The next season, 1980, was enough to give everybody in Denver ulcers. We sank to 8–8. It was tougher to swallow than the Maalox. The Broncos had acquired Matt Robinson from the Jets, and that was supposed to turn our offense around. But he was terrible. We had wasted two number one draft choices on a guy with a weak arm. It didn't take anyone long to figure out that he was no help. So we had to keep going back to Craig. We were blown out in Philadelphia in the opening game, and that set the tone for the season. Not only were we not going back to the Super Bowl, but there was no way we were going back to the playoffs.

I was wondering if going to the Super Bowl had been an accident.

The team was sold. That came as a shock to all of us. We never thought Phipps would get out. But along came Edgar Kaiser, Hein Poulus, Grady Alderman, and Dan Reeves, a whole new cast of characters that none of us knew anything about. I sat down and talked with Hein and Grady, and I knew right away we had trouble. Grady's only function as general manager was to get coffee for Hein and Edgar. Hein had never seen a football game before, and he was the guy negotiating the contracts. He told me it didn't matter what I had done before, and I said: "Wait a minute. That's all I've ever been told. All that matters is what I've done before." He said they were starting all over. This is the same crowd who told Randy Gradishar, Hall of Famer, that he should take a generous cut in salary. If it was laughable before, it was downright hilarious now. Bob Swenson and I held out as a package deal for a while, but we finally had to give in. I love football too much to sit out. But after that, football became even more of a business, especially with the Kaiser crowd around. They didn't care for the players or the fans. Denver got the raw deal.

And then we had Dan Reeves, who brought the so-called innovative Dallas offense and the Tom Landry attitude with him. Even though Dan had been a player, he didn't act like it. He was certainly not a players' coach. He had this offense that nobody understood. He told us it would take three or four years for everyone to understand it. That did the defense a lot of good. We knew we would have to continue to carry the team, and we knew we would get old and lose most of the players while Reeves was experimenting with this great offense nobody understood. Sure, it confused other teams. But it confused our own team even more.

Finally, a couple of years later, a few of the players, leftovers from the Dirty Dozen, sat down and talked about Reeves's lack of a relationship with his players. Louis Wright was our player rep, and we sent him to Reeves. Reeves, I think, was close to killing Louis. But they talked for a while, and Dan actually started to understand. He changed from that day forward. He would listen to us. He would joke more with us. He became a human being. He finally got out of that Dallas Cowboys' plastic mold. I think he had a lot of growing up to do as a coach those first couple of years.

Like Red Miller, Reeves discovered the defense in 1981, his first season. So he played it close to the vest and hoped the defense would hold up. We brought in Steve DeBerg to try to replace Craig, but Craig was the man they continued to go to. The quarterback was older than the coach.

In the final game of the season we go into Chicago 10–5 with a chance to win the AFC West championship, a chance to regain our ground. The defense is really geared up, and the offense goes out and stinks up Soldier Field.

It was humiliating. Craig was throwing interceptions everywhere and fumbling. He should have pulled himself. The fans pelted us with snowballs and called us everything imaginable. It was the ultimate humiliation. I remember that like it was yesterday. I had played football so long to earn respect, and we had none. There are times when you just can't put up with that anymore, and I just wanted to show those asses who we really were. But we couldn't do it. We couldn't win. Maybe we deserved to be pelted with snowballs.

I felt like we were back to square one. It seemed we had spent the whole season backed up against our own goal line, with games close and scores low. We were always just trying to hang on.

The situation sank from desperate to hopeless during the strike year, 1982. We were 2–7, and I don't even remember winning those two games. I do remember a game we lost, out in San Diego. I was really pissed at the Chargers. In 1975, at a meeting of all the head coaches, it was decided by a "gentleman's agreement" that they would not teach "picking," a defensive technique. But San Diego coach Don Coryell apparently didn't believe in being a gentleman. Picking, for those who may not be familiar with it, is the tactic of obstructing or blocking a defender's path to his coverage—picking him off his man. You can do it legally in basketball. In fact, it's a great move in basketball. But in pro football you're not supposed to do it. And we were victimized in the San Diego game by three picks that ended in touchdowns. Twice I went to the refs, and all I got was that old Chico line: "Hey, man, it ain't my job." After that game I was determined to kick San Diego every time we played them, and we usually did.

But that year we were embarrassing, whether we were picked or not. There were some hard feelings between the players and management, and there were hard feelings between us and Dan Reeves. A coach is management, no matter what he says.

The strike was a miserable failure. That's when you start to look around and think. I didn't know whether it was time to quit or go someplace else or punt. It was getting to be SOS—same old stuff. We had great expectations but nothing to show for it since the Super Bowl.

But just when I was on the verge of throwing in the towel, I turned on the TV one day during the off-season and heard John Elway's name. He already had been acquired from Baltimore, and he was already signed, sealed, and delivered.

John Elway was a member of the Denver Broncos. Hallelujah. There must be a God.

We had drafted an offensive lineman, Chris Hinton, and it looked like we were headed for another year of misery. Suddenly, now, we've got John Elway, the golden boy, the kid who was supposed to be the new Joe Namath.

It gave us hope.

I really think Edgar Kaiser was trying to save himself with the signing of John Elway. One of the things I've found out over the years is that, no matter how bad the players want to win, they won't win unless the owner knows how to win. If the owner isn't interested, enough things can be screwed up so the team doesn't win. Edgar had been called every name in the book. His reputation wasn't worth squat in Denver. Owning a football team started out being fun for him. He could wear a Broncos' T-shirt and pick up women, telling them he owned the Broncos, and he was the Big Man on Campus for a while. He could snap his fingers and get the best table in any restaurant. But after we lost, and after the stuff came out about Hein and Grady and their incompetence and the way that Edgar kept raising ticket prices and sticking it to the fans, he was a leper. He couldn't get a table next to the kitchen. He must have figured he had to do something. So he acquired John in exchange for our backup quarterback, a couple of draft choices, and Hinton. And we had to play the Colts in two exhibition games so that Irsay could make a ton of money off the deal. Just goes to show you.

I'm sure Edgar thought about selling the team. But then came this chance to get Elway and be a hero again, and he did. Plus, Elway would improve the value of the team. I understand Kaiser made a fortune—$20 or $30 million—from the Broncos in the short time he owned them. This was the same guy who didn't want to pay me a few thousand bucks more to play.

And a babe shall lead them out of the wilderness. Young John was our light at the end of the tunnel. I was realistic enough to know that quarterbacks don't imme-diately come in and win big. It was going to take three or four years, and I didn't know if I could hang on. Our linebacking corps was breaking up. Joe Rizzo was gone. Bob Swenson got hurt. Randy would retire soon. It wasn't the same anymore. We had been hurt, frus-trated, and pissed off for so long. The defense had been on the field for so long, for so many years. When all is said and done, I will have played more plays for the Denver Broncos than anybody in history, offense or defense. I don't need the statistics to back up that claim. I've played in more games than anybody, and the defense was on the field for more plays than the offense for the last 14.

We thought John might keep us off the field.

Training camp was funny that year. John took the pressure off everyone else, but there was plenty on him. There were dozens of media people every day wanting to talk to John. They had an "Elway Watch" in the newspaper. He couldn't go to the toilet without someone following him. I felt sorry for the kid. I took him aside a few times and told him not to let it get to him. But he handled it well for a rookie. I don't believe anybody else since Namath has had to go through the stuff John did.

There were all the questions about who would start, Steve DeBerg or Elway. DeBerg had better statistics and more experience, and he could read defenses. But, of course, John was going to be the starter. The players knew it. There was never any doubt. One look at the guy, and you could tell he was something special. In training camp I stood with my mouth open. Now I know what the trainers must have felt like when they watched a young Cassius Clay box. I have seen the best.

It wasn't going to be easy, though. In the first regular-season game in 1983, John got knocked out, threw a couple of interceptions, but came up with enough plays so that we could win anyway, 14–10. Then the next week we went to Baltimore, and it was the worst I've ever seen it in my whole life. The fans were brutal. They threw things and spit on us, and I don't know how John survived. They screamed things at him I'd never heard before. And he's screaming in the huddle because nobody can hear him, wide receivers are on the sideline saying they have no idea what play is being called.

They're just running any old route they can think of. But somehow we managed to win. We managed that way the whole year, winning nine games and becoming the wild card team. The one game I really remember was the rematch against Baltimore late in the season at Mile High Stadium. To have any chance at the playoffs, we had to win. But there we were in the fourth quarter with time running out, and we had the ball on our 25, losing 19–14. Everyone remembers The Drive in Cleveland in the AFC championship game, but John Elway came up with a great drive for us that day against Baltimore. The four linebackers were on the sidelines, and Randy looked like he was meditating. Jim Ryan shook him and said, "Randy, I think we're going to win this game." Swenson looked at Ryan and said, "I think you are crazy." But the offense slammed down the field, and we won 21–19. John was beginning to show that he had a golden arm.

There were three teams from our division in the playoffs—the Raiders, the Seahawks, and us. And we had to play in Seattle on Christmas Eve. Boy, we've had some terrible games in Seattle. It's the noisiest stadium in the league, and they just always seem to get so fired up to play us. And we got our butts kicked bad. We were never really in it. It was Randy Gradishar's last game. Nobody believed he was going to retire, but I knew. Randy and I had been rooming together, which was somewhat unusual. Most often, blacks room with blacks, and the white players stay with white players. But there was no color line between me and Randy. We were like brothers. The night before the game we stayed up talking about his career and mine, and I knew he wanted to get on with his life. But this was a terrible way for him to leave the game. On the sideline at the end Randy was crying. I would know the feeling.

The plane ride home was long and bumpy over the Rocky Mountains. When you lose, the flights always seem twice as long, especially when it's the last game of the season. There was a blizzard back in Denver. We got home just after midnight, Christmas morning. Nobody was there to greet us at the airport. We had fallen a long way since 1977. Ho, ho, ho.

I didn't like the pattern. It was the third time since the Super Bowl year that we made the playoffs, only to lose on the road. Were we ever going to win another playoff game?

My ability wasn't falling off, I didn't think. But you're probably the last to know. For some players, it just goes in a hurry. I've seen players in this league just disappear. We picked up a running back several years ago who had once been great. Suddenly, he didn't have a thing left. We got a defensive back once who had been All-Pro. All of a sudden, he was finished. Then, there are those who just glide on. Look at Charlie Joiner. If you saw him five years ago and compared him to last year, you'd probably notice a difference. But year to year, Charlie Joiner seemed to be the same. I never noticed that he was slower or couldn't catch the ball as well. But after last season he announced he was retiring. I guess we all have to figure out when the time comes—on our own.

After John Elway's first year I tried to calculate how many years I had left and how many chances I would have to get to the big game. I had no clue, but I felt we would get closer as he got better.

1984 was a strange year. We played great defense again, scored a bunch of touchdowns on defense. We pulled out games we shouldn't have won, and people thought we were doing it with mirrors. For example, in the opening game against Cincinnati we won 20–17, but I don't know how we did it. John Elway got knocked out of the game, Gary Kubiak came in, and we were just barely hanging on at the end, with the Bengals driving for the winning touchdown. On third and 10 at our 40 with less than a minute to go, Kenny Anderson dropped back, and we were in trouble. Half of us were in a zone and the other half in a man to man. When they snapped the ball, I was busy shouting to Steve Foley. I was just trying to get somebody to cover the tight end. I had looked down the line and seen that nobody was on him. My job on the play was to stick to the running back, but, when I couldn't get anyone's attention and when I saw the tight end veering off in the middle, I took off after him. At the last possible second, just as Anderson threw to M. L. Harris, I dove headlong and just barely got a hand on the ball. But I was able to knock it down. And we won the game. It really is a game of inches. If I hadn't noticed that our defense was screwed up, and if my fingers were an inch shorter, they would have had the first down and at least a field goal to tie or a touchdown to win. But they didn't, and we were riding high, and it felt great to know I could still make a big play when we needed it.

The second week of the season we got blown out at Chicago. The next Sunday, we were trailing 14–0 at Cleveland, and Bob Swenson and I were on the sidelines talking about something that had nothing to do with the game. He was hurt and in street clothes, and he was telling me about the cheerleaders in Atlanta or the price of some stock.

"Bob," I said, "somebody's got to do something, or we're going to get blown out again." Well, the second I say that, Hanford Dixon, a defensive back for the Browns, chased John Elway right over to where we were standing. There was no reason for him to be shoving John when he was out of bounds. So I took a poke at Dixon and drove him toward Swenson. Swenson pushed him back to me, and I proceeded to grab Dixon around the throat. By the time Swenson and I finished working Dixon over as a tag team, he regretted treating Elway the way he did. There were offsetting personal foul penalties on the play, but after the fight the Bron-

cos had a new attitude. It was Swenson's best move of
the season. Bob and I fired them up. We went ahead and
won, 24–14. They didn't score another point. You do
whatever's necessary to protect your teammates. But
the coaches told Swenson to stay farther away from the
sideline.

My best personal game was against New England.
I've always played well against the Patriots, and there's
really no good reason. I don't hate them. In fact, I've
had a lot of friends who are Patriots. Anyway, late in the
third quarter, I knocked down a pass intended for
Stanley Morgan. On the next play I made the tackle on
Craig James, and I was at the bottom of the pile. I got
up to see where the ball carrier had been stopped, and
I suddenly felt a pinched nerve in my back. I came
hobbling out, but a play later I went roaring back in.
Tony Collins came my way, I guess to test me. I stopped
him cold at the line, and we stopped their drive. And we
beat them 26–19.

Nothing could be finer. We're 13–3 and cream of the
AFC West, and we go to Seattle at the end of the year,
and we have to win, and we've had problems there all
the time, and we beat on them pretty good, winning 31–
14. We charge into the playoffs with all the enthusiasm
of a champion. We're going back to the Super Bowl. We
really thought we would be playing the Raiders for the
AFC championship, and that's the way I wanted it. But
Pittsburgh beat them. And then the Steelers dominated
us like we hadn't been dominated all year. And at our
stadium, too. We couldn't blame it on the artificial turf
at Three Rivers Stadium. The Steelers run on us,
control the clock, get the big plays, and, in general, just
beat us. We thought we were so much better than they
that we wouldn't have to put out the kind of effort we
did in Seattle. It doesn't take long in the NFL to find out
that, if you don't play as well as you can for 60 minutes,
you get beat.

To get over the heartbreak of losing another playoff

game, I took an unusual off-season job. I worked as an intern for Senator Ted Strickland at the state capitol. I was sort of investigating politics as a second career. Who knows? It could happen. Look at Jack Kemp. And Bill Bradley. Gerald Ford played football. And President Reagan was the Gipper. Senator Tom Jackson. Has a ring to it. That intern job opened some more doors for me. Plus, I wanted to see what a true democracy was all about. In football it's a dictatorship. But one day I had lunch with a bunch of the senators, and I found out their lives could be just as screwed up as a football player's.

I was beginning to feel like Colorado was my home. I had made the Pro Bowl three times, but my best individual honor came in 1984 when the Colorado Sports Hall of Fame named me Colorado's Pro Player of the Year. What made the awards dinner doubly exciting was that one of my best friends, Billy Thompson, B.T., who had retired from the Broncos and owned a Mc-Donald's franchise—all the free burgers I could eat—was also inducted into the Hall of Fame that night. I don't think we stopped celebrating for a week.

We had another great year in 1985, 11–5, but no cigar. Didn't even get to the playoffs. I will say this: the offense was coming along. As a defensive player you start to appreciate the unbelievable abilities of a John Elway. You start to think, maybe this kid has the kind of heart and intestinal fortitude to make it big. I see him week in, week out, and he gets knocked down, and he gets right back up. You can see the toughness and the leadership qualities.

The opening game of the season was an indication that 1985 would not be our year. We played in Los Angeles against the Rams, and Eric Dickerson wasn't even with the club. He'd been holding out, so they turned to Charles White, who hadn't had a big rushing day since he left Southern California. The guy could

barely make it in the league. But he went berserk
against us, over 100 yards, and they beat us 20–16.

I missed that game because I'd hurt my knee, and I
was on injured reserve. August 21, 1985. That was the
day. Arthroscopic surgery. I hadn't suffered a bad
injury since my rookie year. They tried everything in
camp to get my leg to come around, and nothing short
of surgery would work. Luckily, the injury didn't turn
out to be too bad, and I was back in the lineup by
October. We played Houston, and I wanted to pop the
first white jersey I could find. I had to know if my knee
would hold up. I got hit hard and wound up on my back.
It felt great. Not the hit, the knee. When you're coming
back from a knee injury, you don't want to be tentative.
I actually played a lot more in the game than I expected
to, but I think the coaches wanted to see what kind of
shape I was in and if the knee would blow out. They
were beginning to wonder if it was all over for me.

"Tom Jackson is exactly what you want in a professional. He's a throwback to what football players used to be like. He would probably play the game for nothing. That's what I told him when we were negotiating his contract.

"I remember when Edgar Kaiser owned the team and had a fishing trip in Canada. Tom went along, and there he was in the boat talking with the presidents of a number of major companies, and he was the most comfortable man there. I think he could have become the president of most of those companies if that's what he set out to do."

John Beake,
Denver Broncos general manager

11
DON'T BURY MY HEART AT WOUNDED KNEE

Don't stop the world. I don't want to get off. I'm having too much fun.

I wasn't even supposed to be around for 1986.

But they weren't going to keep me off the team. No way.

I had two goals left: to play in more games than any other player in the history of the Broncos and, more important, to go back and win the Super Bowl.

In October, against Seattle, I reached one of those goals: I played in my 183rd game. I had surpassed a couple of my best friends, Barney Chavous and Billy Thompson. I'm sure my record won't hold up forever, but it stands for something. It means that for a fourth-round draft pick that everybody thought was too small to play in this league, I hung around for a while and got to play a lot.

But I'll never forget picking up *The Denver Post* one day in early February, and this headline was staring me right in the face: "T.J. won't start for Broncos." There was no other T.J., so they had to be talking about me.

"Tom Jackson, the Denver Broncos' veteran defensive leader, is no longer the club's starter at right outside linebacker," the story began. This was news to me.

"Ken Woodard, his backup for the past few seasons, has been elevated to starting status in anticipation of the 1986 season, according to the club's defensive coordinator, Joe Collier."

Think the Broncos were trying to tell me something? Otherwise, why in February, five months before training camp, would they announce who was starting at linebacker? Sounds rather suspicious, don't you think?

I was so pissed. You'd think after all the crazy years I deserved to have someone come to me and tell me before throwing it out in the newspaper.

There's no doubt they wanted me to retire. The word had come down from Dan Reeves and Pat Bowlen. I was making a pretty big salary, around $350,000 a year plus some deferred money, so they could save some money there and maybe hire a couple more scouts and assistant coaches or get a new whirlpool or Bowlen could buy another house.

They didn't believe I could come back off the knee injury. The doctors said the knee was arthritic, so there wasn't a whole lot they could do with it. It had just been worn down.

But they didn't even have the balls to tell me in person what they were thinking. That's typical in football. Haven Moses was one of the best receivers the Broncos ever had, and Dan Reeves put him on waivers toward the end of his career because he thought nobody would take Haven and because he wanted to save a spot on the roster for a younger player. One of those cute moves. Well, Dan tried to hide it from Haven, who heard about it on a radio talk show. That's cruel. Imagine finding out you're fired on the radio while you're driving to work.

OK, if that's the way they wanted to play, I would play by their rules. The Broncos didn't figure I would, or could, rehabilitate the knee. They were subtly telling me to retire. But I had come too far to get this close to the Super Bowl again and give up. So I made up my mind to work harder than I ever had before. Maybe that newspaper story was supposed to get me pissed off and make me go to work. It did.

I had been written off, literally. Everywhere I went, people kept asking when I was going to announce my retirement. They made me feel like an old man. I was only going to be 35 in 1986. In most businesses you're heading toward your peak at 35. In sports, you're too old. So tell that to Pete Rose or Jack Nicklaus or Kareem Abdul-Jabbar. I knew my skills hadn't diminished.

By March I still hadn't met with Dan Reeves personally to find out what he was thinking, but it didn't matter. I publicly said I was coming back. I told the press: "I'm doing whatever is necessary for me to play football this coming year. . . . I still think I'm a damn good football player. I'm not ready for the junk pile yet."

Trainer Steve Antonopulos and I set up a rigorous off-season program, and I started on it in the spring, going to the practice field every day and working out three times a day. I concentrated on wind sprints and weight-lifting and box drills to strengthen the leg. The box drill will either get you well or get you dead. You stand next to the box and do 30 or 40 repetitions of jumping on and off that box with your legs together. Try this at home, and you'll know what I'm talking about.

Another thing I did was drop my weight from 231 to 223. Sure, I've lost some quickness over the years, but losing 8 pounds I'd been carrying helped me gain back some of my speed, and I had the feeling I was a lot faster. Mentally, I felt as good as I did physically.

In no time I could see how much stronger my leg was getting. And I could feel more power in my upper body. I had never been that active during the off-season—I was used to spending the off-season in Hawaii, but the game had changed a lot since I was a rookie. Now you're almost forced to make it a year-round job. If you sit, you're gone.

When training camp started, I could tell the coaches had mixed emotions. There's nothing worse than the feeling you get when the coaches think it's time for a veteran to leave. A distance, a wall, goes up. They wanted me to do well, but they thought it was time for me to step aside and let Woody—Ken Woodard—take over. After all, he was regarded as one of the team's best athletes. He could run a 40 in 4.5, and he was good. But he wasn't as good as me.

I know the coaches were trying to figure out what to do. They pushed Barney Chavous out the door, made him retire, and I was next.

I was playing too well, though.

Myrel Moore told me one day after a meeting: "You keep this up, and they can't let you go. They'll have to start you. And I'll fight for you."

The most difficult part of my rehabilitation had nothing to do with the physical problems or the mind games with the coaches. I had to test that knee. You never know until you're hit. No matter how much you work out, there's going to be a point where you have to have someone hit the knee.

Of course, the knee was never meant to play football. If God intended for us to play football, he would have made a knee that swings four ways. But the knee is supposed to bend only one way. And when it's hit hard and forced to go in another direction, you've got real trouble. Ask me. Look at what happened to me in the Super Bowl. For the want of a knee, the Super Bowl may have been lost. But it's the risk you take. If you're going to be in athletic competition, you have to sacrifice your body to the cause. The boxer risks brain damage because he's been hit in the head too often. For a football player, the problem is the knee. Artificial turf certainly has aggravated knee injuries, but you could put concrete out there, and we'd still play. You see a lot of ex-pros who can barely walk; Dick Butkus, for instance. You want to cry when you see him walk. And Dan Reeves—he had operations on both knees, which are all but gone. I'm sure when I'm 65 I'll be able to tell you when it's going to rain, and I'll need one of those walkers or a wheelchair. It's not very promising.

So I was especially thrilled when, in training camp, I started getting knocked around, and my knee held up just fine. I was my old self.

On August 22, 1986, the headline was a lot different from the one in February: "Veteran Jackson retains starting LB job."

Take that.

I had done it. The old war horse had proven them wrong again.

"Linebacker Tom Jackson apparently has won his training camp battle with fifth-year challenger Ken Woodard to be the Denver Broncos' starting right outside linebacker when Denver opens the regular season against the Los Angeles Raiders just a little more than two weeks from now.

"That much became clear through the last four weeks of the Broncos training camp in Greeley," the story said.

"I don't think there will be any change in that area for a while," assistant head coach Joe Collier said on Thursday.

"This is the best Jackson has looked in the last three or four years. When he came back and started getting involved in our off-season program last winter, you kind of had the feeling he was going to come back pretty strong."

Myrel Moore, my coach, said: "I think T.J. came through the training camp in a much better position than I thought he would be, physically and production-wise. I was quite pleased."

If they had been trying to motivate me to get ready to play, they won. If they were trying to run me off, they lost. Either way, I was the big winner. And it was just the beginning.

"Tom Jackson was born to play in the Super Bowl."
Buddy Martin,
The Denver Post *columnist*

12
RAISE HIGH
THE ROOFBEAM

I was tired of being on the verge. We were always on the verge of something, and that doesn't mean a damn thing.

We had a great training camp in 1986, maybe the best since I'd been with the Broncos. Training camps are designed to break your spirit. They're like Hell Week in college fraternities, but this Hell Week lasts about eight weeks. And they're probably a lot like basic training in the army. I'm sure that's where the idea originally came from. Bust your ass, and you'll be prepared to go off to war. The coach wants to push you past the point that's your limit. It destroys your will after a while. You just want to get it over with. The coach wants you to feel real down, and then he wants to see how you play football at that point. When you're at your worst, how will you perform? It's a strange game. They treat you like children. They even put in a curfew. And the funniest thing is that the players *need* a curfew, so what does that make us?

Every publication I bought in Greeley picked us to go to the Super Bowl. *Inside Sports, Playboy, Sports Illustrated, The Sporting News.* I'm sure *Hustler* and *Field & Stream* probably picked us, too. We couldn't get too cocky, but at least we were being recognized around the league. John's picture was everywhere. Plus, the defense had a fresh attitude. We were coming together after some real controversy. Steve Busick, who had been our starter at inside linebacker since Randy retired, was traded to make way for Ricky Hunley, the high-priced kid Pat Bowlen traded for. Barney, of course, was gone, and Rubin Carter was splitting time in the middle. We made some other changes and picked up Mark Haynes, who had been an All-Pro with the Giants. And we were more aggressive now. We were doing some things like the Bears had the year before. We used to sit back and wait for teams to make a mistake. Now we wanted to force that mistake right away. Also, it used to be that your best 11 players played every play. Not anymore. Like so many other teams, we were substituting for situations. We'd put in six defensive backs. Nickel, dime defenses.

I felt good. Let's go.

Word association, 1986 season:

Denver 38, L.A. Raiders 34—good news, bad news. I was glad that we won, angry that I didn't play. I was introduced as a starter, but that was the extent of it. I was in the game early when the Raiders got a couple of first downs. Woodard was run in, and that's the last time I was on the field. I watched the Raiders put up 34 points against us, and I didn't play. Everyone was celebrating, but I didn't feel very good. Maybe I was being selfish, but if I had been in there, the Raiders wouldn't have scored 34. Everybody in the world knows how well I play against the Raiders. But they forgot about me. Just pushed me over to one side. I was fuming. You don't treat somebody like that. After the game I talked with Myrel Moore and told him I didn't appreciate what they did to me, that if they were going to play Woody, go ahead and start him. But don't mess with my mind. Myrel apologized and calmed me down, and it was forgotten. I went home and drank a whole bottle of wine by myself and went on with my life.

On a brighter note, it *was* a great feeling to beat the Raiders. They're not as good as we are anymore. We have the horse. We have a Pro Bowl quarterback, and they have a quarterback who belongs in a bowling alley. It's almost sad. The Raiders aren't anything anymore. They're just average. We scored 10 points in the last quarter to come from behind and beat them. It always feels good to get that first one out of the way.

Denver 21, Pittsburgh 10—Monday night game. A team we should beat. The Pittsburgh Steelers aren't the Steelers of old. John threw three TDs, and they didn't even score a touchdown until late. I remember once on Monday night TV when Pittsburgh scored 42 on us. But this game will be remembered for the refs' screwup. John Elway lateraled to Gerald Willhite, who threw a touchdown pass to Steve Watson, who was so wide open I could have caught the ball. But the refs ruled it a double forward pass. The new instant replay showed that Elway lateraled, but the replay guy wasn't allowed to say anything because that kind of play wasn't covered under the new rule. This kind of thing doesn't bother you quite as much when you win by a comfortable margin.

Denver 33, Philadelphia 7—considering that it was Buddy Ryan's first home game as the Eagles' coach, you've got to understand that this was an excellent win for us, in Philadelphia. Overall, maybe our best team effort of the year. For the first time in a long time we had a running game. Sammy Winder got 104 yards; Gerald Willhite had 91. Since I've been in Denver, way

back in the Dark Ages, we never ran like that. Three and
0. Mike Harden intercepts and runs for a touchdown.
He was also our leading tackler, which is good and
bad—good for him, bad that a cornerback leads us in
tackles. That usually means they're getting past the
front seven. Strange things are going on defensively.
Ricky Hunley started the game on the bench because
Joe wanted to open with a 4-3. Rick Dennis was in the
middle, and Woodard started on the weak side in place
of me. Here they trade Steve Busick so they can play
Hunley; then they don't start him. They also replaced
Rubin Carter, who has been at noseguard forever, with
Greg Kragen. Everything worked this time, but I don't
know. You don't go screwing with a good thing.

Denver 27, New England 20—tough football game. I
was very impressed with New England's team, but I
was even more impressed with our ability to come out
in the second half and bounce back. A lot of people
wondered what happened to us in the locker room,
what the coaches did to us. Did they beat us with chains
or something? Not really. People think there are mira-
cles that go on between halves. I haven't heard one of
those fire-and-brimstone speeches since I was in high
school, except from John Ralston. Dan Reeves isn't like
that. Doesn't matter whether we're ahead or behind. He
says the offense has to do this and the defense this and
the special teams this, and we go on about our business.
Dan is not a rah-rah kind of guy.
    We got serious and started executing better in the
second half. I was really fired up. I even started a couple
of fights. Sometimes to get your teammates going you
have to get into some extracurricular activities, I've
found. They respond. We're the only team in the AFC
undefeated, 4-0. The last time we were 4-0 we went to
the Super Bowl.

Denver 29, Dallas 14—just a figment of the old

Cowboys. America's team, ha! We don't have any incentive to beat them anymore. Most of the guys from the Super Bowl year are gone, and we don't see the Cowboys that much. But Dan has incentive because he had been a player and coach under Landry and wanted to beat him bad.

They started Steve Pelluer because of Danny White's injury. I don't think a whole lot of Danny White, but Steve Pelluer is nothing to write home about. We sacked him five times and intercepted him three times, and it was pretty workmanlike. Tony Dorsett didn't play, and it was my first opportunity to play against Herschel Walker. He was nothing special against us. I wouldn't put him on my list of top 10 runners. He told us he had problems figuring out all the shifting we threw at him defensively. We do keep running backs confused. They can't figure out the holes ahead of time. Joe Collier said afterward that we had blitzed more than he'd ever seen. We're still undefeated, but we're trying not to get our hopes up. We're trying to remain calm.

Denver 31, San Diego 14—outclassed them. We were on a roll, feeling very confident. We had the ball for 39 minutes on offense. That makes such a difference to the defense. Mike Harden is having an All-Pro year. He intercepted another pass for a touchdown, and we kept Dan Fouts under control. We've always had Danny Fouts pretty well figured out. We went through a period of years when he couldn't do anything off us. We saw in the films that, whenever they were going to pass, he would line up with his right foot back just a little. If they were going to run, his feet would be side by side. It was a giveaway. Finally, Dan figured out what he was doing, but it was fun while it lasted.

There were rumblings that, unless the Chargers beat us, Don Coryell would be gone. And he was. He supposedly resigned, though I imagine he was pushed out. But I had a good feeling about John Elway. He came back from his worst performance, against New England, to riddle the Chargers, and afterward he said he could see us getting to the Super Bowl. A lot of people didn't want him talking like that. But I like my quarterback to brag if he can back it up.

New York Jets 22, Denver 10—6-0 going into the Monday night game and feeling pretty good. We weren't thinking about going undefeated, but I noticed some of that stuff in the press and heard some fans talk about it. We've got three talk shows in Denver, and everyone's got an opinion about the Broncos. Broncos this, Broncos that. Most of the players listen to the shows and talk about what's being said about them. But I don't listen to the shows. It's not that I'm not interested, but my car doesn't have an AM radio in it. I can't listen. And up where I live I can't get most of the shows, anyway.

The Jets were about to make sure we didn't go undefeated. We walked into a buzz saw in New York. In the first half we made every mistake possible, and we were down 22-0 at halftime. It's hard enough to come back from that against any team, including the Little Sisters of the Poor, but we had no chance against the Jets that night. We just needed to get out of there without getting hurt. It's just too bad it had to happen on national TV. But we were still 6-1. And the one thing I've learned over 14 years is that you can't do anything about losing. You can't bring it back. Once you strip off your gear and take a shower, it's time to forget it and go on to the next game.

I just wish we could get some punting. Our punting game may kill us before the season's over. Jack Weil was awful, and now they've brought back Chris Norman. If Norman was any good, they wouldn't have cut him in training camp. Norman never got one over 40 yards. I'm sure he was nervous, though. He's got to make it right away, or he's gone. Kickers are a strange breed, anyway. They stand over at the side of practice, balancing the ball on the end of their foot. And get paid for it. I like Rich Karlis, our placekicker. He reminds me a lot of my paper boy.

Denver 20, Seattle 13—Seahawks come in thinking they can tie for the division lead, but our character shows. This is the first time we've had to bounce back from a loss, and we take it to them pretty good. John set a record with his sixth 300-yard career game. He's got it going. This is the quarterback I've always wanted on my side.

Some of the names this season seem strange to a guy who has been around. We picked up Freddy Gilbert to go with Andre Townsend, Greg Kagen, Tony Lilly, Randy Robbins. It's the Pepsi Generation. Where have you gone, Joe DiMaggio? Where have you gone, Joe Rizzo? Sometimes I feel like I'm playing with my sons. Some of these guys were in the first and second grade when I came to the Broncos.

We got the big score on another trick play—Elway to Winder to Sewell to Elway and a pass to Vance Johnson. Touchdown. We have some fun with those trick plays in practice. Most of them never work. I wonder what book Dan Reeves is getting them from.

Denver 21, Los Angeles Raiders 10—they've got the most valuable running back in the league, and we've got the most valuable quarterback. Our QB can pull the trigger, and he prevails over their running back. Marcus Allen is the best, but he doesn't have much to work with offensively. Mike Harden had another touchdown return, and we got six turnovers. That's the kind of defensive effort that reminds me of 1977. Maybe destiny is on our side again. I told the press when the game was over: "We were in the driver's seat before this game. But before today we were driving a Continental. Now, we're driving an 18-wheeler."

San Diego 9, Denver 3—rude awakening. We score no points. It's a fact of life in this league. If you don't score a touchdown, chances are you are going to get beat. We got beat. It's kind of scary. For several games we had offense, but when we need it here, we get nothing. We scored only three points against the team that perennially gives up more points than anyone else in the league. And San Diego plays a third-string quarterback and beats us. Tom Flick. Wasn't he a cowboy in the movies? And what about our punting game? This time Norman dropped the ball on a punt, and San Diego recovered. We have to go back to work.

Denver 38, Kansas City 17—a hard week of work paid off. We bounced back again. We heard a lot of harsh things about us during the week, but we exploded for 31 points in the first 19 minutes. As bad as our punting has been, we finally found something good about it: Chris Norman threw a touchdown pass out of punt formation. Maybe he should have been a quarterback, because he sure can't punt. We got another touchdown on Gerald Willhite's punt return, and the defense scored one on Andre Townsend's fumble recovery. That's a balanced attack. One for the defense, two for the special teams, two from the offense. My roomie, Ricky Hunley, got his first interception. I told him it was about time. At that rate he's getting about $500,000 for each interception he makes.

We have a 9-2 record, and the Jets are 10-1. I'd like to play them again in Denver. In the NFC the Giants and Chicago are both 9-2. That could be your final four, I'm thinking.

New York Giants 19, Denver 16—the Giants. Maybe you've heard of them. We should have won this game. Their defensive end, George Martin, makes a great defensive play, stabbing John's pass with his arm and picking the ball off and running it back for a touchdown. We battle and battle and get back in it at the end, but we blow a coverage defensively, and we lose. In our minds, though, we knew we could beat these guys. I remember walking off the field and thinking that I'd love to get another chance to play them.

Denver 34, Cincinnati 28—great football game. I would have loved to sit in the stands and watch this one. Cincinnati has a left-handed John Elway in Boomer Esiason—they both have a lot of spirit and heart. The Bengals wouldn't quit; they came back with two touchdowns in the fourth quarter. You feel a lot better about winning a close one like that against a good opponent than you do when you just go beat up on somebody like Tampa Bay or Indianapolis.

Also, great news on the home front. We got a new punter, Mike Horan. He punted three out of bounds inside the 20, and Cincinnati fumbled another one. And he's left-handed, like Bucky Dilts, who was our punter the Super Bowl year. The 75,000 at Mile High Stadium gave Horan an ovation on his first punt. We were cheering on the sidelines, too. "God, that makes me feel good," he told me on the sideline. "A week ago I couldn't buy a job in football, and now people are giving me a standing ovation for a 45-yarder."

Kansas City 37, Denver 10—going into Kansas City with a chance to win it all: the division, the home field advantage. Apparently, we lose sight of that. Offensively, we turn the ball over too often, and defensively we're garbage against the throwing game. We leave the field doubting ourselves. We no longer feel like that 6–0 team earlier in the year. We're not going to get to the Super Bowl playing like this. John was sacked five times, and they got 20 points on us in the fourth quarter. Not a sterling effort.

Denver 31, Washington 30—a game we needed. The Broncos may not be the most talented team in the league, but we sure do have togetherness and charac-

ter. When we beat the Redskins, we knew we had
overcome the *crème de la crème* of the NFC. If they
aren't the best, they are among the top two or three.
And they had to have that game as badly as we did. Rich
Karlis kicked a 32-yard field goal in the last few
minutes to make the difference. Mike Harden had two
more interceptions. Some people said he was too slow to
play cornerback, and he's taken a lot of grief over the
years because he's a safety playing out of position. But
this season he's jammed it in their faces. The man had
a Pro Bowl year, but, once again, it just proves that the
players aren't so smart. Mike was the best cornerback in
the league, and nobody voted for him. And the Broncos
tried to replace him by bringing in Mark Haynes.
Haynes, a Pro Bowler, had some contract problems
with the Giants, and when he came to Denver, he kept to
himself. He never did become a part of the team, and I'd
be surprised if he is with the Broncos for very long.
Especially with the way Harden continues to play.

Seattle 41, Denver 16—must we even discuss this
game? Maybe we should. As it turned out, we needed
this to get us into the right frame of mind for the
playoffs. It's said that you have to be peaking just before
going into the playoffs, but in this case, losing so bad
was a slap in the face that made us get serious for New
England. Curt Warner humiliated us. He rushed for
about 200 yards and put on a show. Seattle can beat
you like that in Seattle. There's something about that
Kingdome. It's the only domed stadium that I think
gives a team a decided home field advantage. I've never
had any problem with noise in other domes. Let me
make a prediction: if Curt Warner stays healthy in 1987,
the Seahawks will be a Super Bowl contender. I think
you're looking at a team that could make it real rough
for us to win the division again.
    In this game, though, we were lacking some emo-
tional intensity. I don't think I've ever seen Dan as mad

as he was after the game. He told us: "If you're the damn champions, you should play like champions, damn it." He was boiling. One of the newspapers got a picture of me sitting on the bench with my mouth shut. One of the other players said that might have been the first time in my life I had kept quiet. There's not much you can say when the score is 41–16.

So we were 11–5 and headed to the playoffs. You might have wondered if we belonged after the shellacking we took in Seattle. But the playoffs are a whole new season.

EX LIBRIS PEGASUS

"T.J. is so high-strung the night before a game. He can't sleep. What's funny is that the coaches made me and Tom roommates because they thought he would settle me down, mellow me out, and take some of the wildness out of me. Tom's a lot wilder than I am.

"You have to respect Tom. He came into the league making $25,000, and here I am making $600,000 or something. It was a big difference, but he played his heart out. Didn't matter what he was making. I hope some of Tom's attributes do rub off on me."

Ricky Hunley,
Broncos linebacker

13
WHEN YOU COMIN' HOME, ORANGE RIDER?

We had a serious problem on this team. We had become too soft, too complacent.

So I met with Dan Reeves after the Seattle game.

"We've got to get back to the tough practices, Coach. We need to start hitting again."

"You're right," he said. "But we've backed off on the hitting because we had so many guys hurt." It was time to forget about injuries. A bunch of our players needed a good, swift kick in the butt. Someone needed to tell this team and this town that when we don't play well, we lose. We've never been a dominating team, like maybe the 1985 Bears, who would have a bad day and still win. If the Chicago Bears don't play well, they're still good. When the Denver Broncos don't play well, they stink.

Now, with that in mind, I know how we will have to play against New England.

We had another problem, though. Clarence Kay had left the team earlier to go to a rehabilitation program because of his drug problem, and now he was back, eligible for the playoffs. Dan called me and the other captains in and asked our opinion about whether he should activate Kay or Rubin Carter. I felt Rubin, who had hurt his knee earlier in the year, deserved to be added to the roster. Now, we may not need another noseguard, and Rubin might not even play, and Kay's a great blocker and all that, but this would be Rubin's last year, and he deserved to go out in style, not go out on the injured reserve list. It didn't seem right. But the offensive players wanted Kay back, because he's such a great blocker. I realized after the meeting that Dan already had his mind made up; he was just trying to soften the blow. He had planned to bring Kay back, and he did. He hadn't announced it earlier because he was trying to keep the furor down during an important week, but when he called us into that room, he already knew. Coaches are like that.

I saw some quotes in the paper from our guys, who said: "We're going to win no matter what." Yeah, we're going to win no matter what, if the other team doesn't play as well as we do. And New England was playing well. They looked super against Miami, and they looked good against the other two teams we had on film. Big play potential. I looked at my notebook over and over, and what it kept screaming to me was: "Stop Stanley Morgan, win the game."

Stanley Morgan makes New England work. Great wide receiver who can take over a game the way a good quarterback or a running back can. Not many wide receivers can dominate a game, but he can.

We had a very special session Saturday morning before the playoff game. Dan got up in front of the team and said he had been talking all year. Now he wanted to hear what the players had to say about this game. I found out later he got the idea from Chicago Bears coach Mike Ditka, but that didn't matter. It was something we needed. I stood up, the old veteran, and spoke first. I told the team that, a lot of times, you believe that because you're young, you're going to be in this situation again, which makes one playoff game seem less important. I've been in the game 14 years, I said, and I've been to the Big One just one time. For me, this will probably be the last time, so don't screw it up. If we go out and play hard, we'll be successful.

A lot of guys got up and talked about 1984 when we were 13-3 and lost at home to the 9-7 Pittsburgh Steelers, who weren't nearly as good as we were. Jim Ryan went back and did an account of all four playoff games in his eight years. He said he'd like to *win* one playoff game before his career was over. It was an amazing meeting.

By the time we finished, everybody, I mean *every* player, had spoken, talking about how tired he was of hearing the Broncos were lucky and how this game would be the start of a tradition of winning. We could have played the game right then and there.

When I got to the stadium Sunday, I was bubbling over. Probably my last game in Mile High Stadium. I appear to be looser than anyone in the locker room. Being the wily old veteran, I don't want anybody to think I'm nervous. There's been so much attention placed on me, and everyone keeps asking if this could be my last game. I don't know. I'm playing so well. I want to get the season over and then decide what the future is.

Nobody did anything out of the ordinary in the locker room, just those little superstitious things you see every week. I've got my own superstitions. I always get taped by the same person—trainer Steve Antonopulos. Then he and I do the spatting on the shoes. Just before we go out, when Dan gives us our final talk, I go over and shake John's hand, and I shake Gary Kubiak's hand. It doesn't hurt to shake Kubiak's hand. If John gets hurt, Gary's the guy we depend on. I've seen it too many times: a quarterback gets hurt, and suddenly you have to depend on a guy who maybe hasn't played in months. I think Kubiak's job is the second hardest on the team.

Once the game draws near I stand on Reeves's right during the national anthem, and during the pregame prayer I hold hands with him and Pat Bowlen. And the last thing I do is shake Steve Antonopulos's hand before I go out on the field. It's a tradition that started years ago. The trainer is the most important man as far as I'm concerned.

I was as emotionally keyed up as I've ever been for a game. And when they called my name, I really did think of all the times Randy Gradishar and Bob Swenson and Joe Rizzo had run out on the field before me, and I said: "Guys, this is for all of you." Billy Thompson and Rubin Carter and Barney Chavous, all the guys I'd played with who had gone on.

The defense played well right off the bat. We stopped the Patriots all four times in the first quarter, and everything was going our way. Tony Eason was having problems early. He was shaky. At one point, Eason was getting ready to throw to Stanley Morgan, and Mike Harden stepped right in the way. Eason tried to hold up his pass, but the ball slipped out of his hand and hit the dirt. He had totally misread the defense, and I think that kept him confused. Twice he threw into coverage. That one play had him thinking all day.

Meanwhile, John had one pass picked off, but not to worry. We came right back and moved down the field for a field goal. Then, Stanley Morgan catches a pass for 36 yards, and they're down the field for a touchdown. Don't let Stanley Morgan beat us—that's all I've been thinking—but he's beating us, and we're behind. Oh, shit.

Everyone is straining to stay cool. That's what we've been taught. But panic is drifting in. And I'm trying to find out what went wrong on the touchdown play because I was in coverage with Tony Collins and didn't see it. That happens all the time. Something big happens, and you don't see it because you're busy taking care of your own problem. The only time a defensive player sees a big play is when it happens against him. And it happens on offense, too. I've talked to one of our offensive linemen, Keith Bishop, about it. He said he has no idea what's going on on the field. Offensive linemen just do their job. They block, then a few seconds later they find out whether the quarterback had completed the pass or not. The position I really wouldn't want to play is cornerback. When a defensive lineman is beat, it's usually for a few yards. When I'm beat, it's a first down. But when a cornerback is beat, it's a touchdown. And everybody knows it. They show the instant replay from 15 different angles, and you always see the cornerback lunging or falling down, and the receiver is spiking the ball in his face. It's like being on the field naked; you've got nowhere to hide.

Elway runs in for a TD, and we feel better, but I am thinking this game is going to be a roller coaster ride.

Late in the half, New England intercepts a pass and kicks a field goal to tie the game 10–10. And John Elway, The Man, is hurt. I'm glad I shook Kubiak's hand. Actually, I didn't even know that John was injured. When he threw the interception, my job was to get with the coaches and find out what defense to call. Then, in the defensive huddle, someone said John was hurt. I saw them helping him off the field. When we went into the locker room at halftime, I immediately went to the training room, which looked like a MASH unit. There were a half-dozen players being looked after. The doctor said John was going to be all right. John was on the table, and his ankle was being wrapped. I put my hand on him, and all John said was: "I'm going to play, T.J." The panic disappeared. For a while.

These two teams have a lot of respect for each other. Even though it was the playoffs, I noticed guys were helping players from the other team get up. That's unusual. I was called a cheap-shot artist, though, because on a punt I whacked the snapper. He's got his head down and can't see, and I guess the Patriots were taking umbrage. But I was looking for an edge somewhere. I had the feeling at halftime this game was going to come down to one play.

We come out and drive the ball for eight minutes. Beautiful. But those last five yards are impossible. And we can't get the ball in. Field goal, 13–10. We're feeling good. John is OK, and we march the ball right down their throat, most of it via the run, and we haven't been able to run on anybody for weeks. If we can run, we beat anybody.

Whoops.

New England pulls a flea-flicker on us in the third quarter. I had filtered across the field, and I see the toss to Mosi Tatupu, so I run parallel back 15 yards across the field. And I see No. 27 wide open. I just know that Eason is going to Hawthorne. I see him look at Hawthorne and then look somewhere else, way down the field. Wait a minute. If Hawthorne is wide open, and Eason is looking somewhere else, someone else must be even *more* wide open. I look down the field, and, of course, there's Stanley. Then I see Louis Wright, and I know it's going to be close. All anyone can do is stop and watch. It's in slow motion. There's no help for Wright. I saw Wright go up, and I thought he was going to tip it, but he mistimed his jump, and I didn't see Morgan catch it because of the angle. But to my right, the New England bench is celebrating. So we get ready for the extra point. We're letting Stanley Morgan beat us.

The fear is back. We're behind, folks. Four points back. A field goal won't do it.

But John wasn't going to be denied. And one play in particular shows how much he has grown up. He makes New England jump offside. He's great at making teams do that. He can change his cadence better than any quarterback I've seen. A defensive man gets used to a rhythm from a quarterback, but suddenly John changes that rhythm, and 11 guys jump off their toes. So John forgot about the play he called and went for it all because he knew we had a free toss. He can't lose. He got Vance Johnson in the end zone.

At that point the defense stepped up.

We had to get our crowd into the football game. The game itself should have been enough to make them berserk, but the flow of the game was so erratic that they were finding themselves with the same fear we had. So I decided to exhort them to get up. Get up, people. I waved my arms, and they got up. Makes you feel like you've got this great power when you can make 75,000 people rise in unison. This must be how those TV evangelists feel, I was thinking. I wanted a microphone. I was hollering: "Make noise. Do things. Have fun. Make it impossible for New England to hear. Make it impossible for Eason."

I can tell you, when you have the kind of racket we had in the last few minutes, you can break down any opponent. You can try it at home. Turn up your stereo as loud as it will go and then try to concentrate on something like balancing the checkbook. You can't. Our fans are so great when they're emotional.

I thought about my dad at that point. Years ago we were having a conversation, and I was the big-time expert. And he said to me, "Junior, the key to football is pressure on the passer." This from a man who painted water meters. And he was right, you know. We were putting pressure on Eason, and New England went crazy.

I thought we might go into overtime, but our running game was working, and that made them use up their time-outs. And when you don't have time-outs left, you need field position. That's where Irving Fryar comes in. He made the critical error. You don't field a punt on your one-yard line. But we honestly had been waiting for something like that. Our special teams coach, Chan Gailey, had told us in meetings that at least once in the

game Fryar would do a stupid thing like field the ball
inside his five. He always does. Either he has no concept
of the field, or he doesn't care. Twice before, from what
their guys had told me, he had caught punts on the one-
or two-yard line, and fumbled them out of bounds and
lost the ball game. And here he did it again.

They're buried, and right away Rulon Jones sacks
Eason. Safety. I'm thinking they're about on the two-
yard line, and I look up at the clock to see how much
time is left. That's when I see the score change from 20
points to 22. I'm smart enough to figure out what
happened. It's over. When you look back on Bronco
history, Rulon's sack on Eason will stand out as one of
the team's greatest plays. And from a guy who set the
club record for sacks during the year.

We're off to Cleveland for the AFC championship.
Going home. For the last time. It has always been
special for me to play in my hometown. I'm the only guy
on the roster who wants to go to Cleveland.

Wasn't there a line in a movie once? "Hey, Ma, look at
me. I'm on top of the world."

EX LIBRIS
PEGASUS

"One of the greatest moments I've experienced as the team's owner was at the AFC championship game when Tom and I knelt down for the prayer. We were holding hands, and Tom started crying. It was one of the most touching events in my life, to feel the emotion of Tom Jackson. I had to swallow hard to keep from crying myself. Tom will go down in history as the most inspirational player the club's ever had or probably will have. I hope that in some capacity Tom will always stay with this club."

Pat Bowlen,
Broncos owner

14
THE GREATEST SHOW ON TURF, BUT NO JOY FOR MUDVILLE

Thomas Wolfe was wrong. You can go home again. If you take a bunch of football players with you.

The return of the native son.

I was going home to Cleveland for the American Football Conference championship. Boy, that sounded good. Everything was great, but how was I going to find 50 tickets for relatives and friends? Rich Karlis and I are the only players from Ohio, so we're scrambling. But nothing matters. I know we are going to win this game. Cleveland never gave us any trouble, in Denver or in Cleveland. You know how you always have somebody's number. Well, we had Cleveland's. We had beaten the Browns seven straight times.

Cleveland is making a comeback, and I'm not just talking about the football team. The city seems to be coming alive again. I loved Cleveland when I was a kid, but by the time I left, there were some real problems. But now, they are making the effort to make it a viable city again.

I could feel our confidence building on the flight over—everyone was loose. One guy I did feel sorry for was offensive guard Paul Howard. He had joined the Broncos the year after I did, and these playoffs meant as much to him as they did to me because he was probably retiring. But he tore ligaments in his knee in the New England game, and people were saying that his career was probably over. That old gang of mine was disappearing: Barney Chavous was forced to retire before the season started; Rubin Carter was put on injured reserve; and now Paul. That left only me, Louis Wright, and Steve Foley from the last time we played in the AFC championship game. It's been a long time.

I'm the only Bronco who ever lost to Cleveland. Dubious achievement. The last time we lost to them was in 1974, before the other guys got here. It was the first time I played in front of my sister and my father. I was so excited about playing in Cleveland Municipal Stadium and they beat us 23–21.

Some writer in Cleveland said Bernie Kosar was a better quarterback than John. How stupid can you get? Kosar is a good, young quarterback, but he's not in a class with John. This writer said: "One reason I like the Browns is that they have the advantage over Denver at quarterback, the most important position. Kosar is wary, suspicious, looking for danger behind every yard-line marker. He won't show much emotion, although you can see a bit of smoke coming out of his ears. Elway is open-faced, excitable, more likely to get flustered when things go wrong. The type of person Kosar is goofs up less than the type of person Elway is. In truth, Elway is overrated. He has not yet arrived as a first-class operator. The voters must have been dreaming when they put him into the Pro Bowl as Dan Marino's substitute." John said he hadn't read that shit—"I don't like reading about myself"—but I did, and I was pissed.

We flew into Cleveland Friday night, and the ride was rather quiet. I read a magazine on the way over. Louis and Sammy Winder and a bunch of the other guys slept, and John wandered up and down the aisles. His ankle, hurt in the New England game, seemed fine in practice.

Strange things started happening right away in Cleveland. When we got to the Stouffer's Hotel, a few hundred people were standing outside dressed in orange. Naturally, we assumed they came from Denver to wish us well. Wrong. What I took for our orange was Cleveland's *burnt* orange, and these folks were Cleveland fanatics. They were there only to bark and throw dog biscuits at us. I didn't know their defense was known as the Dogs, so I took all the barking to mean they thought we were dogs or something. When I met my sister in the lobby, though, she explained to me what the dog business was all about. It takes all kinds: Orange Crush, Dogs, Purple People Eaters, Doomsday Defense. Seems like every good defense has to have a name. All night long I could hear those people barking.

At the stadium Saturday we practiced in our street clothing. It had become somewhat of a tradition with Dan—he'd let us goof off and relax the day before the game. We would walk through our plays and throw the ball around. Nothing strenuous. It looked funny, though, to see Rulon Jones in a big cossack coat in the stadium.

The Browns had gone to Florida to work out before the game. Probably a good idea. It was cold in Cleveland. The stadium was awful. They had a tarp covering the field, but the sidelines were under an inch of mud and water. "It looked like maybe the groundskeeper had drowned out there," I told the press. I knew conditions were going to be awful. That wind off Lake Erie was already whistling up my spine. I stopped and looked up toward the end zone where my father and I used to sit when I was a kid. There were always those posts that restricted the view from some seats. We usually ended up behind a post, always craning to see Jim Brown. I can still smell the hot dogs. The next day people would be eating hot dogs and watching us beat Cleveland.

On Saturday evening I got to go home, to my old house, and I ate a big meal with family and friends. Even *then* there were friends who took the time to tell me how the Cleveland Browns were going to beat us the next day. My brother-in-law was telling me how Cleveland had come back alive for the Browns, that it hadn't been that way for years. Every building had a sign for the Browns. It reminded me a lot of the way it had been in Denver in 1977. The Browns fans knew there was no way the Browns could lose.

Later, I went upstairs to my old room. My father hasn't touched it. He leaves it just the way it was. A few posters and pictures. I thought about my mom and growing up and the guys on 121st street, and I wondered if they would be watching the next day. And I said: "Mom, I'm going to win this game for you."

Day of the game. The snow flurries picked up just as the game started. Cold and windy. That wind comes in off Lake Erie and swirls around in your face until it starts to burn. They had the tarp along the sidelines, but it was just like walking in a mud pit. Great conditions, huh? The field wasn't much better.

We were harassed the entire time we were there. But I think it gave us an edge, especially when they started throwing dog biscuits at us from the stands. I started thinking what would happen if our fans adopted a similar philosophy and started throwing horseshoes or even horseshit at opposing teams. By the time we got to the stadium, we were infuriated. We warmed up toward the end zone known as the dog house, and I must have been pelted at least 50 times by those dog biscuits. And there's something about that constant barking that can drive you crazy.

But this kind of day was perfect, I thought, for defense. You start thinking in terms of turnovers because of the conditions. It'll be tough to throw and even tougher to carry.

We had spent a lot of time trying to figure out what to do against Bernie Kosar. But Joe Collier finally decided that Kosar had a tough time reading defenses. People think this kid has great composure and knows how to read defenses, but that's not at all what's happening. What Cleveland's coaches have done with him is smart. They tell him that on a certain play this guy is open. If he's not, go immediately to this other guy. He should be open. If neither works, throw it away. So there's no reading of defenses. The Cleveland coaching staff has done a great job of guessing.

So we wanted to take away the first two receivers. We elected, then, to put more guys in the passing lanes and not blitz. We might not get the sacks, but we felt we could confuse Kosar, make him throw into coverage or even throw interceptions. And if we confused him enough, the pressure from Rulon Jones and the other guys would get to him. Kosar had said before the game that he was worried about our defense, and I think it showed.

"The main challenge is that they present a multiple of sets to really make you have to think," Kosar had said. "They mix it up and move around a lot. The main thing I've got to do is not get caught up in what they do and concentrate on what we're trying to do." But we confused the kid.

Defensively, Cleveland played really well. Our offense sputtered, and we missed a couple of good opportunities to get the ball in. At halftime the score should have been 10–7 Broncos or 17–7 Broncos. But it was 10–10, a new ball game. They scored in the first quarter, but we came back with a field goal and a touchdown by Gerald Willhite. And they got a field goal from Mark Moseley. Boy, what a lucky guy he is. Released by Washington. Gets a call from the Browns. Ends up in the playoffs.

Misses a field goal last week that could have won it. Gets another chance. Makes it. And here he is against us, kicking a field goal. I was thinking, I don't want to be beat by this guy if it comes down to that. And it looked like it could be overtime or one of those last-second affairs.

The snow had come and gone, and it was just cold. They said the wind-chill factor was six, and I believe it. You sweat on a day like that, and the sweat just freezes on your face. And you feel like you've been rolling in mud.

What was worse, though, were those biscuits. Gary Kubiak got hit in the head with one, and they were all over the ground on that one end of the field. Muck and slop and dog biscuits.

We had the ball coming out for the second half, and we felt good. We had taken the edge off the Browns' enthusiasm. Before the game they came running out like a bunch of ponies. Now they were acting like players in a difficult football game. Offensively, we didn't change much at half, and it showed. Our first couple of drives weren't anything to talk about. We got a field goal, but we struggled. The only thing that saved us was that they were struggling, too. They got a field goal in the fourth quarter. It was 13–13, and I thought we might be there forever.

The belief was that one big play would win it. So our defense kept talking about how we needed that big turnover. A Mike Harden pick. A fumble recovery. Do something. But we couldn't get it.

Wham! Smitty gets beat for a touchdown. It's like someone hits you in the gut. You can't breathe. We had gone into an X coverage, which is what we got into on third and long, so I wasn't in the game. More backs and more defensive linemen, so the linebackers come out. From the sidelines, it appeared to me that Dennis Smith was going to pick the ball off. I thought Kosar just threw it up. He was getting a lot of pressure, and in that case you throw long in the one-on-one coverage, and even if it's intercepted, that's as good as a punt. In this case, Dennis made a swipe at the ball and got spun around. He's thinking the ball will come outside, but it comes down inside, and Dennis falls down. What a helpless situation. Brennan gets it and takes it into the end zone. Dennis Smith knows the emptiest feeling in the stadium. I've been there. Suddenly nobody's your friend. The whole world has just seen you get beat one on one.

The 80,000 fans begin chanting, "Super Bowl, Super Bowl." NBC is setting up its cameras in the Browns' locker room. Ahmad Rashad has already gone to their locker room, and the championship trophy is in there. The champagne is on ice. The town is ready to celebrate.

We get in our special teams huddle for the kickoff, and Chan Gailey talks about how important it is for us to gain good field position for the offense if we're going to have a chance to win. I'm trying to focus on what I'm supposed to do and not get depressed. I've got to make my block.

Well, I didn't even see the guy I was supposed to block because the ball skidded past our return people. I saw it stop somewhere near the foul line. Ken Bell was apparently trying to run it. Oh, God. He can't get a handle on the ball. The pileup looked like it was on the one-inch line, although we heard later that it was on the two. We walked over the sideline, and the partying in Municipal Stadium got louder.

Our offense came on, and none of them said anything to us. They were fairly disgusted with the field position we left them with. In the huddle Keith Bishop said: "OK, we got 'em right where we want 'em." And the other guys laughed. Keith was just trying to make a joke, lighten things up, because the situation looked pretty ridiculous. "We're huddled up in the end zone," Keith said. "I looked out the back of the end zone, and all there was was photographers and network cameras. I sat there and looked at them, and I thought all they were trying to do was get a picture of our huddle as a bunch of losers. They wanted to get the faces of defeat in their pictures. They were trying to show us whipped, beaten. That's when I decided to lighten things up. And we did." I'll say they did.

We're about five minutes from the end of the game, and five minutes from the end of my career. Dennis Smith was alone, just standing with his arms folded. I know he was thinking that, if the game ended like this, when the team plane headed back to Denver, he would just stay on and jump out over the Pacific Ocean.

The first couple of plays I thought we ought to be throwing the bomb, but we were throwing short stuff. After the first first down, we had some room. A swing pass and a run, and the third down was close. After the second first down, I could see that the Browns were in a deep zone to keep us from getting behind them, which meant they were leaving some seams. And John could see that, too. He made a pass to Steve Sewell just about at mid-field, and I knew we had a chance. Dennis Smith came up to watch. Now he's excited. The offense can take him off the hook. We were using up a lot of time. Dan didn't seem to be concerned with the clock. I kept thinking, Hurry up. But we got to the 50, with two minutes remaining. There was time. Just don't make any mistakes.

Uh-oh. The snap hit Steve Watson on the butt. Steve went into motion, and the ball glanced off him. John makes a great play. Not only does he catch the ball, but he has the presence to throw it to the right spot. He picked up the third and 18. Big play. His demeanor was so calm. John told me later he could tell the ball was going to hit Watson, and he was getting ready to jump on it and take the loss. A fourth-down play would have been even tougher. John came up with an incredible play there.

And then we scored the touchdown, John to Mark Jackson. I was still worried, though. Extra points aren't sure things at that end of the field. Rich Karlis would be kicking into the wind, into the open end and into the "Dawg Pound," all those biscuit-tossing fans. When he made it, I started breathing again. I was sure we were going to win. That drive, under those conditions, was the greatest I've ever been around. To go the entire length of the field in the last few minutes of the AFC championship. Where's the guy who said John was overrated? I had already known that John was a super quarterback, but The Drive convinced everyone else.

I was running out on the field to congratulate Rich for the conversion, when I saw Minnifield of Cleveland attacking him. What Rich told me later was that Minnifield tried to block the point, missed, and ended up lying on the ground. Rich tried to help him up, and he pushed Rich's arm away. So Rich pushed back. That's when I showed up. I didn't want Rich fighting on his bare foot. I knew we would need that bare foot.

So it's tied, and we go into overtime, and I'm to make the coin toss call. I went to Dan for instructions. Last year he wanted to kick off, and it got screwed up. I didn't want to be blamed for a mistake. The wind had died down, but I thought maybe we'd want to kick off and try to hold them. But Dan said to take the ball if we won.

"I don't want to put any pressure on you," Dan told me, "but go out there and win the toss."

I've had a lot of things said to me in my career about stopping players and winning games, but I've never had someone order me to win a coin toss.

I tried to cheat a little and peek under the ref's hand to see which side the coin was on. I figure if heads is up, I'll call tails. I could see the coin, and the tail was up. I called heads, and it came up tails. So much for my theory.

Even though the Browns won the toss, I could see by the look on their faces that the life had gone out of them. They were finished. That drive had beaten them.

They spent the whole overtime still thinking about how they let it slip away. It's a cliché, but we literally had our backs against the wall and beat them.

We kicked off, and I was fired up. My last tackle was the best of the day. I had blown through a gap on third and short. I didn't even see Kevin Mack when he got the ball. All I knew was I hit something. It felt like I hit a concrete wall. If you want to know what it's like to tackle Kevin Mack, go try to tackle your car. Hit your car running at full speed. The car doesn't give. Neither does Kevin Mack. But he went down. Or at least we went down together.

When John came on the field, it was obvious that he had found the groove. First he threw a flag pattern to Mobley. Then he scrambled, vintage Elway, and threw to Watson, and we were close enough for a field goal. I peeked over at Karlis and could see how nervous he was.

"Let's get this thing over right now," I'm saying. I don't want to make the mistake I've seen made by so many other teams. They try to get an extra first down, and they lose the ball. But Dan wanted to run a few more plays. I wanted to go down and tell him to forget it, but I thought better of that idea. Sammy Winder got five yards, and you could tell he was intent on protecting the football. Then we got the ball in the middle of the field for Rich.

I was surprised Cleveland didn't call a time-out to try to rattle Rich. I couldn't watch the kick. Pat Bowlen was nearby, and he couldn't watch, either. He turned around. But I lifted my head at the last second. I had to see it. As the kick left Rich's foot it started to hook. Augh! I couldn't tell from my angle if it would stay inside the uprights. I didn't know if it was good. I focused on the referee.

His hands went up.

Relief.

The field was chaotic. Browns were falling down

everywhere. We had a pileup around Rich. The stands were silent. I decided to get out of there. Mark Cooper had a dog biscuit in his mouth and was yelling, "Arf, arf!" Our beating Cleveland at least meant people at the Rose Bowl wouldn't have to put up with all those crazy dog people and their bones and biscuits.

In the tunnel to the locker room I came upon Stevie Watson, and he said, "Tom, we're going to the Super Bowl." It suddenly dawned on me. Until that moment I hadn't really realized it. Yes, the Super Bowl. Nine years later.

In that tiny locker room, with the pipes running everywhere, you can't move around, and I just stood there and watched. A tremendous sensation. Our equipment manager, Danny Bill, began passing out T-shirts and baseball caps saying "Denver Broncos AFC Champions" and "Super Bowl."

I congratulated my roomie, Ricky Hunley. He had a big interception. As a group, the linebackers had done OK. Woody Woodard recovered a fumble, and Jim Ryan intercepted a pass. When we walked out of the locker room, Ricky had on a coat and tie over his new T-shirt.

When we boarded the airplane, I was trying to explain to some of the younger players what a madhouse it would be in Denver. Most of them had never experienced it. I knew there would be thousands of fans at the airport, and there would be a celebration, and I was excited for the guys who had never gone through that emotional scene before.

There was some talk that the pilots were thinking about going into Colorado Springs to avoid all the people at the airport, but no way was I going to let that happen. The fans deserved to be a part of this. The players asked me to go up to the front, and I told the airline people what we wanted and that we could be very nasty if we didn't get it. The powers agreed with us.

Everyone was keyed up, but we sat on the ground in Cleveland for 45 minutes. Then, finally, the pilot informed us that there had been a bomb threat, and we'd be delayed for an hour.

The final salute from the Cleveland fans.

But we didn't believe there was a bomb, and we partied on. By then we'd heard that the New York Giants had beaten Washington. Even though we had beaten Washington and lost to the Giants, I felt we could beat either one. Dan Reeves said the same thing. I thought New York's defense was better, but Washington had a strong offense. The Giants were playing great in the playoffs, though. What did it matter? We were going to the Super Bowl.

We landed in Denver, and every time we passed a hangar we saw the flight crews waving their flashlights at us. There was the mayor and the governor-elect and thousands of people, and the coach said the captains should say a few words. But by then everyone was bombed. I guess I shouldn't use that word after what we had gone through earlier, but we had consumed some liquor.

I got up in front of the throng and said: "A great deal was made about me going home to Cleveland to play for the championship, but I just want everyone in Denver to know that I didn't feel like I was really home until we got back here tonight. Denver is my home, and we brought the AFC championship home with us."

Not a bad speech for somebody who was totally drunk.

But I was alert enough to remember what we did in Cleveland.

Drive, he said.

"Tom Jackson pushed me. He said some things I didn't think were pretty cool. I can't repeat them. I didn't think he was too classy."

Chris Hinton,
Indianapolis Colts offensive guard

15
THE GOOD, THE BAD, AND THE UGLY—AND THEN THERE'S DICK BUTKUS

EX LIBRIS
PEGASUS

My favorite all-time player was Jim Brown, of course. My least favorite was Jack Tatum.

Near the bottom is Mike Davis of the Raiders. He spits on players. What kind of guy goes around spitting on people? If Mike Davis ever spit on me, he'd be eating that spit out of a straw. Can you believe spitting? It's bad enough you're wallowing around in mud and blood and getting beat up and sat upon and yelled at, but to have some guy spit at you? But that's the Raiders.

Tatum played for the Raiders. It figures. He went out and tried to hurt people. Look what happened to Darryl Stingley. Stingley is permanently paralyzed because Tatum was trying to intimidate him. And Tatum never had the decency to call Stingley afterward. He goes into the locker room and says, "I was just doing my job." Hey, our job on defense is to sack the quarterback and make tackles and intercept passes. Our job isn't to try to paralyze ball players. Now Tatum's one guy *I* might even spit on. I remember when he was playing in college (he was a big All-American at Ohio State and I was a nothing at Louisville), he would knock out somebody every week. I don't mean that he would hit them, and they would limp off the field. He would knock them out cold. Whomp. And they're out. He was a hitter, I'll say that for him. Tatum used to say, "My idea of a good hit is when the victim wakes up on the sideline with train whistles blowing in his head and wondering who he is and what ran over him. I want to punish the man I'm going after." That's sadistic. You can sting somebody, but you don't try to hurt him.

Jim Brown was the best—on the field. Of course, when he was off the field he was dropping women out of second-story windows, but we forgot about that in Cleveland when it was game time. Brown was so big and so fluid. He would go over people, around them, through them, whatever it took. I hate the fact that I didn't get to play against him. We used to wonder why he got out of the game when he still could have played for several years. Now I know why. My body has arthritis, my knees are screwed up, and if the statistics are correct, I'll die before I'm 60. Football does it to you. But Jim Brown got out before his body was totally wrecked.

My other favorite player was Dick Butkus. Oh, he was the best linebacker there ever was. He and the Bears came to Denver at the end of his career and the beginning of mine. His knees were gone, but he made 18 tackles and single-handedly tore us up. I was awestruck. But look at him today. He can barely walk. Nobody will ever match Butkus. He set the standard for all linebackers.

A lot of the people I admired aren't around anymore. My heroes were the old-timers who used to play no matter what was wrong with them. I think I've patterned my attitude around a lot of them. Guys like Y. A. Tittle. He was always playing with blood streaming down all over his face. Looked like a wrestler. Bald and mean. And he won. I love tough players. The tough players will win out. Dan Fouts is a throwback. He may play another 10 years. He just hangs in there, reads defenses, and throws the ball where it's supposed to go. A lot of times he'll read the defense before the play even starts. He'll look at your feet and know where you're headed. Tough man to beat—you feel kinda funny out there trying to hide your feet from him. I guess he was just getting even with us for looking at *his* feet and trying to figure out if he was going to pass. They say it's a game of inches, but with Dan Fouts it was a game of feet.

Then there's Marc Wilson of the Raiders, who is almost too easy to pick on because he's no quarterback, but that guy always amazes me. He's like the scarecrow in *The Wizard of Oz*. Every time you sack him, his linemen have to come put him back together. He's so brittle. Then you've got Jim Plunkett, who is the toughest quarterback I've ever played against. He stands back there in the pocket, and you can keep killing him, and it doesn't matter to him. His expression never changes. He throws people off, gets hit, keeps looking, keeps looking, directs traffic, and throws those ugly, ugly passes—underhanded, sidearm, or whatever—for touchdowns.

Dan Marino is a talented quarterback, but I don't think he could accomplish nearly as much with another team. Don Shula is responsible for a lot of what Marino accomplishes. They say—whoever the experts supposedly are—that Marino is a great reader of defenses. I've seen Marino throw into coverages all the time. The receivers come up with some big catches for the Dolphins, and because Marino has such a quick release, he can get the ball there in a hurry. It always amuses me to hear fans and reporters talk about quarterbacks not knowing how to read defenses. They have no idea what they're talking about. They couldn't read a defense if they had to, so how do they know if the quarterback

can read one? But everybody's an expert. And the
biggest experts are in New York. They must let those
Jets fans out of jail on Sunday. They're the worst fans in
the league. They spit on you. (They must love Mike
Davis!) They question your heritage. They throw stuff at
you. They totally abuse you.

And another thing about the Jets: they have the most
overrated quarterback in the league in Ken O'Brien.
Another quarterback who's nothing special is Doug
Flutie. Just as I thought, he's too short. He'll never make
it in this league. Chicago found that out in a hurry, even
if they won't admit it. Flutie has to throw over much
taller linemen, so he throws a floater. A floater is perfect
for interceptions, and he'll never be able to gun it to his
receivers. The Bears better hope Jim McMahon gets
well. McMahon has a lot of mouth, but he has a lot of
arm and a lot of guts, too.

Dave Krieg out at Seattle is an interesting quarterback. You'll get five good games out of him. Then the
next five games he plays like a peewee leaguer. Inconsis-
tency. I hate that in a ball player. You never know who's
going to show up.

I used to think Terry Bradshaw wasn't any good
because he couldn't read defense, and I assumed that
would put him on the bench, especially because Pittsburgh had a great young quarterback in Joe Gilliam.
But the league wasn't ready for a black quarterback,
and Terry got better and better. He developed other
skills, and he had perhaps the greatest supporting cast
of all time. Can you imagine all of the players he had to
work with? Lynn Swann would just go up in a crowd,
like a ballet artist, and come out of there with the ball.
What a sweet team. I loved that Pittsburgh team for
what it could do.

Brian Sipe of Cleveland is highly overrated. He could
only throw the ball 35 yards. After 35 yards it was like
a knuckleball. Nobody knew where the ball would wind
up. He managed to win some, though. The proof of a

great quarterback is winning big games. Stabler, Tittle, Bart Starr, Bradshaw.

Vinny Testaverde is a gifted kid, but he's got to get used to multiple zone coverages. He's got to learn to read defenses, or he could have problems.

Some guys might as well have "I'm scared" stamped on their foreheads. You can see it in their eyes. Tony Eason, when we played New England in the playoffs, looked shaky and nervous at the beginning of the game. Think of how that must affect your teammates when you stand in a huddle and look scared. Eason came around, though. He had injured his shoulder a few weeks before they played us, and we wanted to test him. Before the game we didn't ask which shoulder. We just went after him hard. And the shoulder must have been all right.

I'll tell you a guy who has a lot of growing up to do. The Boz. Brian Bosworth, the kid at Oklahoma who has made all the noise. I'm not that impressed with his football ability. He's a good player, and he could end up being a good pro with some polish. But I'll give him this piece of advice. If he thinks he's going to be tougher than the rest of the guys in this league, he had better get his head screwed on. If he thinks having his hair cut funny is going to make ball players in the NFL shake and shiver, he's got another think coming. Plus, you have to have a kind of respect for authority. If you're in the service, you don't slap the general. Bosworth thinks that some of the things he has said about authority are real cool and make him sound real tough. But they don't. He's going to find out that a lot of people don't like what he says and don't like him. Look for him to get his comeuppance in the NFL.

When I first came into the league, the running backs I most respected were at opposite ends of the spectrum. One was Marv Hubbard of Oakland, a name out of the past. It was in the days when the running game was the number one priority. You could hand the ball to Hubbard 25 times a game, and he would go for 95 yards and punish you a lot more than you could punish him. The other guy I respected was Terry Metcalf of St. Louis. He was more like Gale Sayers. He could catch, pass, run sweeps. Any given year he could lead St. Louis in rushing, receiving, kickoff returns, punt returns. He could do everything.

Walter Payton clearly has established himself as one of the greats. Yet they wouldn't give him the Heisman Trophy when he was at Jackson State because they thought it would tarnish the award, handing it over to a kid who played at an all-black school in Mississippi. Those voters were foolish.

Walter is amazing. He can run around you or over you. He'll show it to you, then take it away. He's versatile. He keeps coming at you. You have to have a lot of heart to run 15,000 yards. That takes some big-time guts.

Now Earl Campbell, he would come out of the backfield with the ball and start looking for you. He might make a cut over here and find you. Yeah, go over there and hit you. But it wore him down. Used him up. He got hurt. I always wondered how he felt on Monday mornings. I always felt bad, but he had to feel awful. We got to be good friends, and I always wanted to ask him how bad he felt after games. I didn't have the nerve, though. But that's the only way he knew how to run, and he'd run right over you, like a truck.

Then you've got Franco Harris. He will be remembered as one of the great backs, but the man always looked like he was running from the Ku Klux Klan. He always seemed scared to me, trying to get out of bounds. Running scared was his greatest asset. He saved his body and stayed around a long time, but to be honest, I didn't think he was a tough runner. Franco ran away from you. Earl ran toward you. Different styles. Both were successful, but Franco stayed around longer.

O.J. was fun to watch. The beauty of his running

would distract me on the field. You get mesmerized. All of a sudden you stop and watch his moves. It didn't matter because you couldn't catch him, anyway. I remember a game on artificial turf in Buffalo: they're on the 30, they give it to O.J., he breaks outside and into the open and gets to the 19 and starts to slow down. We're all taking angles on him, but he knows that none of us can get there before he can reach the end zone. He gears down. He was so confident.

Marcus Allen is a lot like that. He can start on one side and take it all the way back to the other. He did that in the Super Bowl against Washington and went 60 yards for a touchdown on a busted play.

Freeman McNeil of the Jets is one running back I don't care for at all. After every play he gets up and acts like he's hurt. He only wants to play when it benefits Freeman McNeil. In the playoff game against Cleveland he got up limping and went off the field. He thought the game was over, and there was no need for him to have to carry the ball anymore. Suddenly the game's in overtime, and he's back out there brand-new.

One guy who isn't overrated as a running back is Curt Warner. He's Gale Sayers on artificial turf. On natural turf Warner is a normal running back, but put him on artificial turf, and he can make incredible moves, moves you won't believe—O. J. Simpson kind of moves. Warner blew his knee out in 1985, and I wouldn't be surprised if he does it again. I hope not, but he's got to be prone to twisting his knee because of the way he moves. He takes the knee where it's not supposed to go. And while we're talking about injuries, I'm surprised Ronnie Lott of San Francisco is still around. He abuses his own body. His career can't last much longer the way he plays. You can go all out, but you don't throw yourself at people. He punishes himself more than anybody I've ever seen. Warner, though, is about as good as anybody I've played against. When he scored on a long run against us in the final game of '86, it was awesome. When we watched the films, you could hear guys oohing and ahing. That was as good a run as I've ever seen from up close. Well, unfortunately, I wasn't too close.

I really like the backs who can run and catch and throw. And they can do things with their bodies that you're not supposed to do. They're like deer in the woods. They move so gracefully.

You see some running backs come into the league who are scared. Either they don't last long, or they run away so well that they last a long time. Franco. Gary Anderson at San Diego is another example. He always acts like he's running for his life, and if you don't take the right angle on him, he can kill you.

The receivers I like are Charlie Joiner and Steve Largent and Steve Watson. None of them has blazing speed, but all three keep catching the football and scoring touchdowns. Largent is going to the Hall of Fame, and a lot of people would have told you he couldn't play in this league. But he's tough. He has heart. And he has a great pair of hands. Joiner was the best, though. We named a pass route the San Diego Pattern because of him. He ran that same 12-yard curl-in for years and always caught the pass. He made a living off that route. You couldn't stop him. I once gave him the hardest lick both of us probably ever felt. It was like two rams meeting on a hillside. He had a deep cut on his head when he got up, and I patted him on the butt. What I remember is that 10 minutes later he walked out of the locker room—he'd had the stitches put in and his head bandaged—and strapped on his helmet and came right back. That'll make your blood warm. Watching Charlie was like watching a John Wayne movie.

Offensive linemen usually aren't your best athletes— their job is to get in the way and mess up things for the defense. But when you get an offensive lineman who can run and block and is so strong, you've got something special, like Anthony Munoz of Cincinnati. He's the best.

One of my real thrills was getting to the Pro Bowl in Hawaii three times to play with some of these guys. I really believe that I would have been there more often, but a lot of guys in the league wouldn't vote for me because they don't like the way I play, the way I talk, whatever. The players look at that sheet and say, "Tom Jackson. What an asshole. I wouldn't vote for him." What I found at the Pro Bowl is that the great players had small egos. You get better only if you don't think you're at the top. That's what they had in common. What's funny about the Pro Bowl is watching the guys from the Super Bowl championship team. They just can't get up for it. After we lost the first Super Bowl in '77, I wanted to go out in style in the Pro Bowl. The Cowboys just wanted to lie in the sun. What you're missing at the Pro Bowl is not talent, but intensity. You don't want to hurt anybody or intimidate anyone. There's no anger. There's a mutual understanding that this is the best of the best, and for one day you just play for fun.

"Tom Jackson is the epitome of a football player. If I could have one man on my side in anything, it would be T.J."

Rubin Carter,
Broncos noseguard

16
THE GREAT PRETENDER

There was a time in my career when I didn't know if I really was who I thought I was.

It takes some explaining.

See, there was this guy going around telling everybody he was Tom Jackson, but he wasn't Tom Jackson because I was Tom Jackson. But he got away with his con game for years.

He started showing up in the early 1980s wearing a Denver Broncos jersey with a No. 57 on it. Sometimes he even had a Broncos helmet with him. And he always claimed to be Tom Jackson. And people believed him. We good-looking black guys all look alike, I suppose. He was in Cincinnati, St. Louis, Indiana, Chicago, even Oakland. You'd think those people in Oakland would know better.

I saw a picture of him, and he didn't even look like me. He was a lot fatter. No muscle tone. If anybody had taken a good look at him, they would have been able to tell he was no football player. But people are gullible.

He has the same skin complexion, but that's where the similarities ended. He was just a large, black man. But his ruse worked. He would usually find a young woman, a widow or a woman looking to get married, and he, uh, got close to her, using my name. He'd tell her he was in the middle of a contract dispute or that he was hurt and couldn't report to the team. Oddly enough, he was always doing this about the time we were in training camp. I guess he thought I couldn't come after him then or that nobody would notice. Anyway, he would sponge off the lady and borrow money and then tell her he'd pay her back just as soon as he signed his contract or healed up and started getting his salary. He apparently seemed like an honest, sincere guy, a Boy Scout.

Well, angry people started calling me from all over the country, wanting their money back. These people would tell me they'd seen me before and that I owed them money. In fact, when we played in Cincinnati, I had a man come to the hotel where we were staying, and he was convinced that I was the guy he had loaned $400 to. He couldn't understand why a guy in my position wouldn't pay him back. I had to go downstairs to prove to him who I was. Good thing he didn't come to my room with a gun. He might have shot me.

Once in St. Louis, a charity organization planned a large testimonial banquet for this guy who they thought was me. In Cincinnati he actually held a football clinic for a group of kids. He even rooked the *kids*! In Chicago he cheated a woman out of $6,000 over a period of four months. He even made a speech—as Tom Jackson—at a fund-raiser sponsored by a local school for the American Cancer Society. At the end of the speech he passed among the crowd, telling his fans that his luggage, including his wallet and credit cards, had been lost at the airport. He got hundreds of dollars. In Oakland he left a hotel holding a $3,200 tab.

This guy was living better than I was. He had more

money, more women, and seemed to be having more fun. He even had the nerve to hire an agent in San Francisco to line up some speaking engagements.

The NFL finally figured out who the guy was, and he turned out to be a longtime criminal with a rap sheet as long as your arm. They put him away for a while. And they'd better keep him away from me. I'd love to put him in a Raiders uniform and get a shot at him. He's probably off somewhere now, though, posing as Lawrence Taylor.

Or writing his own autobiography.

EX LIBRIS PEGASUS

"We've been Broncos season-ticket holders for-ever, and nobody has ever given me more plea-sure, except for my husband Charlie, than T.J. I love to watch him play."

Ruth Wardin,
Broncos fan

17
MAGICAL MYSTERY ORANGE

People in Denver can be weird when it comes to their Broncos.

The Broncos are so important in their lives. Maybe too important. But you have to love them for it.

Broncomania. It was there before I got to Denver, and it will be there after I leave.

The fans waited so long for a good football team. Too long. And if you remember that this was the team that wore those stupid vertically striped socks in the beginning and almost never won a game, you know what I mean. I didn't know much about the Broncos when I got to Denver, but I knew they had been losers. They won four games, three games, even only two games in a lot of seasons. They didn't have a winning season until the year I got there, which makes me feel pretty good, and, of course, they were never a championship contender. One of the opposing coaches used to call the Broncos the "rinky-dinks" of the old AFL. The Raiders and the Chiefs kicked their ass all the time. I've looked

over some of those scores, and I think that's one of the
reasons I hated the Raiders so much—48–10, 31–14, 51–
0, my God, 43–7, 41–10.

We used to hear all the stories about the Broncos
from the old-time veterans. And you pass the stories
down, word of mouth. Last year I tried to explain to the
young people about John Ralston and some of the
others who were around when I got to Denver, and
they didn't know who I was talking about. Maybe Dan
Reeves was kidding when he said he was going to get
me a rocking chair for breaking the record for most
games. Maybe not.

Lou Saban was run out of town because of one game.
The Broncos played Miami once in Denver. If the game
had been in Miami, nothing would have come of it, but
Lou was in the wrong place. With the score tied in the
closing minutes, the Broncos got the ball, and Lou
ordered them to sit on it—the ball, I mean. The game
ended up 10–10. Lou said half a loaf was better than
none. Wrong thing to say. He was gone. But Lou was
gone from a lot of places. The last thing I heard he was
in Florida as an assistant coach at a high school. And
John Ralston is trying to start another league after the
USFL fell out from under him. Someday, somewhere,
John is determined to get into a championship game.

The Broncos had actually been worse before either of
those coaches got there. They actually turned the franchise around. I believe that the Broncos used to draft
from a copy of *Street & Smith* magazine. Their entire
scouting service must have cost 50 cents. They did draft
Dick Butkus one year and Merlin Olsen another year,
but obviously neither signed with the Broncos. The
Broncos didn't sign a high draft choice until after the
merger with the NFL. Floyd Little was the first first-
rounder who ever made it to Denver.

But the Broncos did win the first AFL game, over the
Boston Patriots. They didn't win many after that. Of
course, that was before the team started wearing

orange and blue. They had been wearing brown and
gold uniforms from some defunct bowl game, with
those awful socks. When we went to the Super Bowl the
first time, Fred Gehrke came in before the game and
brought us orange and blue replicas of vertically
striped socks. He wanted us to have them as souvenirs
to remind us how far the team had come. He also asked
some of us to wear them in the warm-ups. Only Glenn
Hyde did. I wouldn't put those socks on as a joke. But
the early Broncos, guys like Goose Gonsoulin—a great
name—did.

Boy, they went through a bunch of players, especially
quarterbacks. It took a long time to finally get one like
John Elway. Consider some of the names, guys I never
heard of, quarterbacks nobody will remember: Jimmy
Baker, Mickey Beard, Marlon Brisco, Joe DiVito, Mike
Ernst, Scotty Glacken, Don Horn, John Hufnagel, Jacky
Lee, Al Pastrana, Steve Ramsey, Tobin Rote (of course),
George Shaw, Mickey Slaughter, Frank Tripucka,
George Wilson, Jr. Wow. Some of those guys were
playing when I was born. I guess Marlon was the first
black quarterback in pro football, but he eventually
was switched to wide receiver. Tripucka, I heard, drew
plays in the dirt. Steve Tensi was supposed to be a
savior, an early Elway, when he came here from San
Diego, but the results were slim, as usual. The Broncos
have a history of trading for quarterbacks. But only
four actually worked out. Forget the Matt Robinson
deal. I got to play with Charley Johnson, who came here
at the end of his career. He was a player. The deal for
Craig Morton turned out to be a good one, and Steve
DeBerg helped us for a while when he came here. But
the best trade, of course, was for Elway. Maybe that will
make everyone forget the deals for Don Horn and the
rest.

Back in those days only one designated captain could
call a time-out, a rule that caused some problems.
Pastrana was the quarterback in a game against San

Diego—his first start—and the Broncos were driving, with the score tied, in the last 45 seconds. He rolled out to set up the winning field goal with 11 seconds left, but he was hit and knocked out cold. Since he was the only player who could call a time-out, the clock ran out. Those were the days.

They had a general manager who chased footballs into the stands after an extra point because he wanted to save money. I'm surprised Edgar Kaiser didn't have his henchman, Hein Poulus, doing that. Back then, Mile High Stadium really was a baseball stadium for the Bears, later the Zephyrs, whatever a Zephyr is. The land where the stadium sits used to be the city dump. They said it was better off as a dump, the way the Broncos played in the 1960s.

The south stands have always been the really weirdo place, my kind of place. I know Hank Stram hated to play in Mile High Stadium because every time he left the field he was pelted. Of course, that's when he was running up the score on the poor Broncos.

There were some pretty good linebackers over the years. John Bramlett got a lot of attention when he came into the league. I hear he was the real wild man. And he weighed less than 200 pounds. But he was a hitter and ended up finishing second to Joe Namath in the Rookie of the Year voting. John's an evangelist now. Ray May came over to Denver from the Baltimore Colts late in his career and was the big linebacker my rookie year. He instilled a winning attitude in the defense and talked us into holding hands when we huddled as a sign of togetherness. Fred Forsberg and Tom Graham were good. And the wrestler, Wahoo McDaniel. The guy I replaced when he got hurt, Chip Myrtle, was a solid player with Denver for about five years. I got my number, 57, from Bob Geddes. Most people don't know I wore No. 56 my rookie year. And then there was good old Godwin Turk. He went on to become a mortician.

Godwin pulled a gun on somebody in the locker room one day. Strange dude. Finally one day he intercepted a pass, spiked the ball, and dislocated his shoulder. That was about the last we saw of him.

One thing the Broncos did succeed at was shutting up Alex Karras. The first year of the merger, Denver played Detroit in an exhibition. Karras, an All-Pro defensive lineman, said he would walk back to Detroit if the Broncos won. Well, Denver won 13–7. How was the walk, Alex? He had an early start when he got ejected for kicking Cookie Gilchrist in the stomach. Karras said that Joe Schmidt hollered at him when he came to the side: "Why didn't you kick him in the nuts and immobilize him?" I hate to even think of that. Most players are gentlemanly enough to avoid you in that area. Except maybe Conrad Dobler. He would go after any part of your body.

Then there was the game in Houston in 1966 when the Broncos got no first downs. None. I read about a man who tried to commit suicide because the Broncos kept losing all the time. When he pulled the trigger, he missed. He was about as good as the Broncos.

I remember watching Cookie Gilchrist as a kid. I've been told that once he got on a field he was unstoppable. The problem was getting him on the field.

The Broncos were finally getting their act together about the time I got here. They had a pretty good draft in 1973—Otis Armstrong, Barney Chavous, Paul Howard, John Grant, Lyle Blackwood, who went on to play in the Super Bowl for Miami, Calvin Jones, Oliver Ross, me. Whatever happened to John Wood? He was a defensive tackle from LSU who was drafted just ahead of me. He's probably a millionaire now with good knees.

The fans endured some hard times. That's why I think they appreciated the winning when it finally came. They had hung in there, waiting to break out and celebrate. And I don't think anything will match what happened in 1977 and again in 1986. Everybody went insane.

Check this out.

The Broncos have sold out every regular-season game since 1970. How many players other than me can say they played an entire pro football career before a packed stadium at home? When I first came to Denver, the stadium seated about 51,000. They expanded it to 75,000, and that's still not big enough. We could sell 125,000 seats for every game. They've got a waiting list of about 20,000, and Gail Stuckey, the ticket manager, told me once that means about 80,000 tickets, because the average is more than 4 per season-ticket holder. Incredible.

I've heard about people fighting in court over tickets when they get divorced. Somebody was suing somebody else over rights to the Super Bowl tickets. And another lady supposedly advertised that she would trade a $3,000 ring for four tickets.

According to the networks, more than 88 percent of the people who live in Denver watch our games on TV. Nine of the 10 largest NFL audiences during the regular season, plus the top two playoff audiences, were recorded in Denver.

They're devoted, those Broncomaniacs.

Back in 1977, it was mind-boggling. That's when the Broncomania and orange madness really got going great. I saw an orange toilet seat. The bumper stickers said: "I'm dreaming of an Orange Crushmas." People painted their cars and vans and houses and church pews orange. They wrapped their babies in orange blankets. A week didn't go by that someone didn't send me something orange. A rug, a shirt, an orange jockstrap. And we had more mascots than you can believe. Still have them.

We've got the Barrel Man, who wears cowboy boots, an orange hat, an orange barrel, and nothing else. I never looked down into the barrel. There's a woman who shows up at the airport every time we leave wearing a coat that has pictures and autographs of all the players on it. There's another woman who dresses up as an orange rabbit. We've got an orange leprechaun. And no telling what else. It gets weirder and weirder.

After we beat the Browns, people were slapping me on the back and wanting to know if we would win the Super Bowl and if I would marry their daughters and if I would loan them money and anything else they could think of.

If you don't wear something orange in Denver on Sunday, they might hang you. Oddly enough, the only people who don't wear orange to the games are the players. Most of us wear business suits or jeans and an old shirt.

There's a privately owned souvenir shop out by our practice field, and I wandered in one day just to see what they had and maybe pick up a Christmas present. I couldn't believe it. Broncos Christmas ornaments, Broncos neckties, pencil sharpeners shaped like Broncos helmets, Broncos lamps, Broncos pot holders, Broncos snow boots, Broncos shot glasses, Broncos sweatshirts—anything orange with Broncos on it that you could imagine. They even have a Bronco brick made out of foam rubber so that when you get mad at something we do, you can throw it at the TV.

When we got ready to leave for the Super Bowl, the Colorado School of Mines put orange bulbs in all the lights surrounding the school's big "M" landmark. I understand at Winter Park, a ski resort, they had a 15-foot Bronco helmet made out of snow that was spray-painted orange and blue, and one of the ski trails was renamed the Road to Pasadena.

Thirty-five police officers in Cortez, Colorado, drove 200 miles to Grand Junction to buy Broncos T-shirts. One guy tried to start a non-Broncos-fan club but gave it up when his kids started getting death threats.

Hostess came out with a cupcake that was colored orange and blue.

Churches changed the time of their services so their members could watch us play in Cleveland. In at least two churches members of the choir put away their hymnals and put on their earphones to hear the Broncos instead of the sermons. Trinity United Methodist Church decorated its altar with orange flowers, and a large portion of the congregation wore orange sweaters with their Sunday go-to-meeting clothes. At Riverside Baptist Church, pastor David Bruce brought out a portable TV as he prepared to deliver his sermon. Bruce then cut short his sermon, and the congregation scattered. "We praised the Lord and then praised the Broncos," said one of the church members.

Before this season Bowlen installed 60 skyboxes at the top of Mile High Stadium. You have to pay $50,000 for the cheapest. Well, when we played Cleveland, several of the box owners threw parties at the empty stadium. They're staring out the window, and nobody's there. They went there to watch the game on TV, which is what I hear they do anyway when we're home. For $50,000 you can just about buy a condo in the mountains and go up *there* to watch it on TV. But these people are true fans. In an empty stadium they ordered pizzas to be delivered.

During the AFC championship and the Super Bowl, the stores were empty. You could have robbed the whole town, but police said crime was down to almost nothing. Even the crooks like watching us play.

After we beat the Browns, the bars ran out of beer. One guy who owns a sports bar said it was "like New Year's Eve multiplied 10 times." In southwest Jefferson County, just outside Denver, two men ran down the middle of the street, stopping passing cars and shaking the drivers' hands. People shouted the score out their windows, and people taped orange streamers onto their cars and drove around downtown honking their horns.

The team was supposed to do a video—like the Chicago Bears' "Super Bowl Shuffle." And they had already taped part of it when we lost to the New York Jets. That's when Reeves, who actually had helped put the thing together with some people out of Dallas, nixed the video, saying all of us, him included, were spending too much time on commercials and appearances and outside stuff when we should be concentrating on football. Good-bye, video. I could have been the newest MTV star.

It must really pay to be the mayor of Denver. The players got 15 tickets each. Mayor Federico Pena received 10 free tickets and had the right to buy another 60 tickets. Can you believe that? The mayor got 70 tickets, and he couldn't blitz if his life depended on it. I think he was jumping on the bandwagon because he was up for reelection, and it wasn't going so good for him until we helped out. To be seen hanging around the Broncos couldn't hurt his image with the voters. He showed up everywhere we were. I hear he cut short his vacation in Mexico so he could come back and be on stage with us. Every time I turned around he was standing next to me. He was next to me more in a few weeks than Randy Gradishar was in 10 years.

One of our biggest fans, though, was Leon Uris, the famous author of *Exodus* and *The Haj* and *Q.B. VII*, which was *not* about John Elway. He lives in Aspen and has been supporting the Broncos since the beginning. A long time. He came out to Pasadena and wrote about us and the game.

"You see, I'm a Bronco junkie. I have been one for a quarter of a century," he wrote in *The Denver Post.* "I've tried every known cure, but nothing works. There's a lot of people like me in the Rocky Mountains. In desperation we formed Broncomaniacs Anonymous. I've secretly been the president of the Aspen chapter for more than a decade. There was only one person who could help: the doc. He was the only one around whose

specialty was the treatment of Broncomanius Majorus
Footballitis. But his methods were drastic, and I avoided
him until the dog biscuit incident.

"The doc took my case history, turning pale as he
heard the full story.

" 'When did you realize you were going into the final
stages?' " he inquired.

" 'When I tried to spray Aspen Mountain orange.' "
As I told you: weird.

One of the newspapers got a picture of all the Disneyland characters holding up a "Go Broncos" sign. Our
press in Denver had to look for things like that, although they didn't have to look far. There were the four
TV stations broadcasting live from California every day
and, of course, the two newspapers—*The Denver Post*
and *The Rocky Mountain News*. Their newspaper war
goes on. I understand the *Post* had 29 stories about the
AFC championship—I didn't count them—and the
News 27: 29–27. And each paper sent 19 people to the
Super Bowl. That's one for every 2½ players. Between
those guys and the mayor, I couldn't turn around
without one of them being next to me.

The Broncos were allotted 20,000 tickets for the
game. That's the front office, not the players. But about
250,000 people from Colorado wanted to go. Some got
tickets from travel agents who put together trips, and
others paid up to $1,000 a ticket, I heard, from scalpers.
I met a guy during Super Bowl week who had two
tickets. He was trying to decide whether to go to the
game or sell his tickets and use the money to fly to
Hawaii and watch the game on TV. That wouldn't have
been a tough decision for me if I hadn't been in the
game. Sell the tickets. The day of the game, back in
Denver, more than 1,000 people showed up at the Hyatt
Regency for a party, and bars were full all over town. I
was thinking about the folks back at Sydo's in Morrison, where I go to eat three or four times a week,

watching on the little TV over in the corner. Morrison was shut down for the day, I'm sure. And it was like that throughout the state. The National Western Stockshow, one of the biggest and best rodeos in the world, is held in Denver every year, and it just so happened that the show's biggest day, Sunday, was the same day as the Super Bowl. Well, the attendance dropped off significantly. The ski resorts tried to have Broncos specials, but it didn't work. Breckenridge had only 3,000 skiers, compared to a normal Sunday of 8,000. I understand that while one lady was giving birth, her husband held her hand and watched the game.

Everybody wants to make a few bucks off the Super Bowl, but a Chicago cabdriver took a bath. I understand this guy came to Colorado on Sunday to sell "I hate New York" souvenirs, but nobody was buying. He was trying to raise enough money to go skiing, but lost about $700.

I was too busy during the first part of the Super Bowl to keep up with our fans, but after I got hurt, every once in a while I would look over at that sea of orange across the way. Toward the end of the game, though, the sea had become a small pond of orange. Most of the Broncos' fans had gone. I don't blame them. They had come a long way, just like we had, and were leaving disappointed.

And when the game was over, Denver was silent. Nobody honked horns. Nobody celebrated. Everybody went home. Life goes on.

Later I saw some of the letters about the game, and one of them pretty much summed up my feelings: "It was a great season, but it lasted 30 minutes too long."

Other people wanted to get rid of Reeves, Collier, Karlis. They probably wanted to shoot me, like an old, worthless horse.

"Has Joe Collier ever heard of the blitz?"

"I'm glad I bought a big screen rather than go to the Rose Bowl."

"I've been a Bronco fan for a long time. I must say that I'm sad, first of all, and most of all very embarrassed."

"I think the game was played too conservatively."

"What did the Giants pay the referees?"

"I think the Denver Broncos played a really good game, and I think it's too bad that the people on CBS could not recognize the fact that Denver could even play a game. They really gave Denver a downplay right from the beginning."

"Tough game. Tough loss. But I still love my Broncos. And I still love the Broncos' fans."

Leon Uris concluded by quoting Adlai Stevenson: "It hurts too much to laugh, but I'm too old to cry."

Then he added that the Broncos "played their best and deserve our love. They all did well by us with their classy behavior. . . . They were class gentlemen, and I'll have them on my team anytime.

"Even in a sport mad country and a sport mad world, the Bronco fans are a phenomenon, and it is painful to see our heroes so badly brutalized."

Amen.

EX LIBRIS
PEGASUS

"A lot of players won't talk to the media, or if they do, it's at their convenience, and most of the time they don't have anything interesting to say. Tom will search you out and talk to you, and it's always good stuff. I probably wouldn't be where I am today without Tom Jackson. Where am I?"

Ron Zappolo,
KCNC sports anchor

18
TOM TERRIFIC AND THE CHOCOLATE FACTORY

If I were the commissioner of the NFL (which doesn't seem very likely since we can't even get a black head coach), the first area I would do something about is the officiating. I'd make officiating in the NFL a full-time job, like it is in every other sport. Aren't the officials in the NFL as important as the umpires in baseball? Well, it's not a part-time job for umps. Here we are working full-time, and we've got guys who sell life insurance showing up one day a week to determine our fate. Most of these guys are too old to know what they're doing out there. Their reflexes are slow. I like a few of them, but the one that gets me is Ben Dreith, who is from Denver. We don't get him too often, which is good. Every time I see him, he says: "How you doing, B.T.?" He still thinks I'm Billy Thompson.

I think I'd make a great commissioner. I'd let quarterbacks wear headbands with anything written on them.

What I'd really do is put a premium on winning for the owners. Give winning a meaning and give the owners a financial reward for winning. For every game played, the owner of the winning team would get more money. Right now, there's no incentive to win during the regular season, and if you don't believe me, look at the Super Bowl. A lot of owners know that if they reach the Super Bowl, all the players will be back the next year wanting a heck of a lot more money. After the Chicago Bears won, everybody wanted a bigger chunk of the pie, which is only natural. Owners look at that situation and don't want to deal with it. In the rare situation, you have an Al Davis, who doesn't mind paying whatever it takes to win. But most of the others are nervous about going to the Super Bowl. So if an owner got 10 million bucks for winning the Super Bowl and $50,000 every time his team won a regular-season game, you'd see a lot of intense games. Right now, though, I think owners would rather play it safe.

I would try to intercede with regard to some of the prejudice I still see in the league. There *is* a subtle racism. Like with black head coaches. We used to say that if you looked down the middle of a field, you wouldn't see a black player. White quarterback. White center. White middle linebacker. White free safety. A lot of truth in that. Name more than one or two black centers. Name more than one or two black quarterbacks. And so on. The same thing used to be true in baseball—catcher, shortstop, second baseman, center fielder. Isn't that strange?

I don't think teams are so afraid to hire a black head coach. I think they're more afraid to fire one. Practically all coaches are going to be fired someday, and the negative publicity around the team that fires a black head coach may be too much for some owners to have to deal with. But they've got to be bold.

In terms of the game itself, I'd like to see the bump rule taken out. Of course, that's my own prejudice. Right now you can bump a receiver only once, and in the first five yards. I don't know why you shouldn't be able to bump him going down the field. You're all equal football players until the ball is in the air. I'd also like to see the in-the-grasp rule taken out. I understand the team's investment in the quarterback could be millions of dollars, but in most cases I don't think the QB is any more valuable than anyone else on the field. Everybody ought to be playing under the same rules. I know the old-time quarterbacks don't like the grasp rule. Billy Kilmer said to me that the referee makes a judgment as to who's in the grasp. Well, what is "in the grasp" for Billy Kilmer may not be the same as it would be for John Elway because of John's ability to get away.

You can keep instant replay, but you're going to make mistakes. That's been proven. As long as you've got a man upstairs making the decision, you're back to a subjective decision. Some of the kinks have to be taken out. I'd get sharper officials in the booth looking at the screen. Most of the ball players say, "If the instant replay helps us, it's good. If it hurts us, it's bad." The instant replay helped us in one game, and I thought, Boy, I'm glad they have it. Then it hurt us, and I wished we'd never heard of instant replay.

The fans are just as divided on replay. But fans are as goofy as ball players. Take ours in Denver. Please. No, you know I don't mean that. They're nice fans, and I do mean that. You can come here as a visiting fan and sit right in the middle of the Denver fans, and you won't be beat up. They won't abuse you if you have on your Cincinnati hat.

I think a lot of people feel that if they pay $10 or $25 it gives them a license to pour beer on the next fellow or act like complete idiots. The ones at the Jets' games do, and you already know how I feel about them. Keep them away from me. If I were the commissioner, I'd fine every one of them.

I still have a picture in my mind, though, of going to Baltimore with John Elway after he had refused to play there. As we were going off the field, I saw police officers billy-clubbing the fans, who were incredibly rowdy. That was the only time in my life when I was scared to death on a football field. I wasn't scared of the other team. I was afraid somebody might try to shoot John, miss, and hit me or one of the other players. We didn't know what the crazies might do.

Fans everywhere spit, throw things, and talk about your mom and dad and ethnic background. So I never like playing away from home. Give me Mile High Stadium for every game, and I would have been happy.

I don't like artificial turf even though it makes me faster. It makes everyone seem faster. But you can get hurt faster, too. You just deal with it.

I don't like playing in San Diego and Washington because their fields are dirt painted green. I don't like the Kingdome because of the noise. On the other hand, I love the Coliseum in Los Angeles. There's an aura of the Olympics. You always feel important in the L.A. Coliseum.

It's always miserable in Kansas City. The wind whips through there, it gets cold, we're always playing there in December, the wind chill factor is 42 below, and there's nobody in the stands. How are you supposed to play in weather like that? I can't have fun at 42 below, unless I'm inside by the fire. Your hands are numb, you can't sweat, and you just do the best you can. That's no 120 percent kind of day.

Atlanta has the best cheerleaders.

But every hotel has become the same, except the Islandia Hyatt in San Diego. Every room has a view overlooking the water, and you can get lulled to sleep there. Otherwise, I just like to get in bed, turn on the tube, and rest. Order room service and keep the drapes closed. Real glamorous.

The funny things that happen on the field help you keep your sanity in this game. Steve Largent came to Denver a couple of years ago, and he caught a pass on the sidelines, but the ball popped out. We recovered it just before a ballboy threw another ball out on the field. And Largent fell on that one. He was showing the ref his ball and screaming that he had recovered the fumble, and I told him: "Steve, we've got the real ball." To this day he doesn't know what happened.

You can't play in this league without dealing with the press. The writers have always been kind to me, and I've been a member of the media myself. I did a show on Channel 9 in Denver for a couple of years. Channel 9 had lost both the Broncos' coaches show and the preseason games to Channel 4, so they came up with their own show. Butch Johnson and I did it together in 1985, but I never felt very comfortable about it. It just didn't work very well. So I moved over to Channel 4 and did a Saturday night show with Steve Alvarez called "Bronco Beat." We did some crazy things. We had a "Wheel of Fortune" game one night. We showed what the players would look like if they were bald-headed. We had a lot of fun with that show. I also had a syndicated radio show for a while. I talked with other players and did commentaries about injuries, rules, the inside of the game. And I wrote a column for *The Denver Post* for a few years. It appeared on Tuesdays, and I gave my opinion of the games: "T.J.'s Corner." I don't think I want to go into the newspaper business. I couldn't afford the pay cut. But I loved trying the different things. I love the challenges.

Mostly, though, regarding the press, I can take 'em or leave 'em. There are good reporters and bad reporters, inconsiderate reporters.

Joe Namath had it right: "I've never seen a sports-writer face a blitz."

Some reporters think of us as being real stupid. The ones I get along with are the reporters who treat me like a human being. But I've found that if you treat reporters like shit, you're the one who will look like shit when the story comes out.

What amazes me in Denver is how the newspapers

write about the Broncos. Way too much. It's not like this
in other cities. Nobody could want to know some of the
things they ask us. Maybe it would be different if
Denver had a major league baseball team. But when
the Broncos are playing, there's nothing else. "What did
you eat this morning, Tom? Did you chew every bite?
Did you go to the bathroom afterward? Did you brush
your teeth? They want to know out in Lakewood."

And it's tough to walk around in the locker room after
a game. You might get killed by a TV station. They're all
fighting to get every little bit of information. I was
flipping the dial during the news after one game and
saw myself being interviewed on every channel. It was
like being the president. And I really didn't have anything to say, which is unusual for me.

Dan had some problems with the press when he got
here. He was accustomed to watching Landry deal with
the press in Dallas, and what Tom Landry says in Dallas
is law. Dan was used to that, but he couldn't get away
with that in Denver. He would cut players from the
team and try to keep it a secret, and it would be on TV
or in the newspapers the next day, and Dan couldn't
understand. He thought he could keep the stuff out of
the media. He thought all the media guys were assholes,
and it's only been in the last year or so that he has come
around.

The media can have a lot to do with your success,
though. Those guys have power. But most of them can't
read defenses.

I try to be kind to everyone in the media, just in case
one of them ends up being the NFL commissioner. If I
don't get the job first.

"I'm going to reveal the one thing about Tom Jackson that nobody knows. He has memorized the entire dialogue from the movie *Arthur*. He knows every line Dudley Moore said. That's Tom. He's fantastic. We'll go to the grocery, and what would be a 10-minute trip normally ends up being an hour and a half because Tom has time for everyone. I've never seen him rude or insensitive to anyone."

Diane Schram,
Jackson's friend

19
ME AND ARCHIBALD ON THE NEAR SIDE OF THE MOUNTAIN

Archibald is this man's best friend.

Archibald's my golden retriever and my companion in the mountains. A friend gave him to me, and we get along great. When I talk, he has to listen. He pays absolutely no attention to what I say, though. A real smart dog. If I tell him to sit, he rolls over. If I tell him to get the paper, he plays dead. But he sure can blitz. Archibald's a year and a half old and a dirty shade of chestnut, and we love each other. He's my family.

Now you know all the inside juicy gossip about Tom Jackson. My home life isn't that sparkling. Just about everything revolves around football.

I have a house in the mountains outside Morrison, a small town just west of Denver. I'm about an hour from Mile High Stadium, and it's perfect. Archibald and I listen to a lot of music together. I read, and he eats. Some of my most contented moments are with Archibald. I don't worry about the bright lights and big city anymore. I always wanted a comfortable house off by itself, somewhere to go off to, and that's what I have. I could spend the rest of my life in this house. I looked around at maybe 25 houses before I found this one, and finally they showed me this three-bedroom, ranch-style house. It's a typical Colorado mountain home. The house isn't extravagant, just nice. It fits me. There's plenty of room for me and Archibald.

I've got almost four acres and a whole lot of trees, a place to get away from everything, including the Raiders.

The house has the things I always wanted—a hot tub, a great kitchen, a fireplace, nice furniture, a big-screen TV, a satellite dish, and a refrigerator. What more could a guy want? I've got my office where I can get serious. My favorite room, though, is my music room. I've got speakers you wouldn't believe, inside and outside the house. I love to listen to Kool and the Gang, especially *Victory*; Lionel Richie; Earth, Wind and Fire; Anita Baker, and, of course, the Rolling Stones. You can always go back to the Rolling Stones to clear your mind.

One thing about this place is that people can't just drop by. Where I used to be, friends would always be coming over. But since I've moved here, it takes a real effort. I love Denver, but I love my privacy, too. And Morrison is the kind of small town I never grew up in. I can stop at the Morris Grocery and learn the latest news and buy some food for me and Archibald and write a check without worrying about someone checking my ID. The people in town treat me like everyone else, and I appreciate that. Small-town people are so genuine.

Being alone used to bother me, but now I cherish it. I always had to be around people, always had to be doing something, going somewhere. Not anymore. Maybe it's maturity. But I can lie here on the couch in my house and listen to music and read and watch the fire and watch the snow fall outside the window, and I'm very content.

I love to relax and play chess. Several of my friends and I have started tournaments, and I've gone through three of those chess computers. I'm pretty serious about the game. Either I'm pretty good, or these computers aren't that smart. I just bought a new computer and put it on the highest level and beat it soundly.

I have a great relationship now with a beautiful lady, Diane Schram, beautiful inside and out. I think Archibald is jealous. To me, marriage has to have the feeling and emotion and companionship my mom and dad had. When it does happen, I want it to be permanent. You don't go to a judge and simply end it. That's why I probably have not gotten married yet. I want to be certain.

Diane and I don't have a glitter-world existence. We spend time with a few friends, eat a chili cheeseburger, and talk. They won't make a movie out of my lifestyle, but that's the way I like it.

There is a downside to living in the mountains: if you want a pizza delivered, it takes about two days. And I do get trapped occasionally by the weather. I wouldn't mind, except when we have a game. Once we were headed to Los Angeles to play the dreaded Raiders, and I couldn't get out. Finally, one of my neighbors came up here with a plow and dug me out. Otherwise, I might have missed the game on account of snow.

I get to Denver every once in a while—an old teammate, Ron Egloff, owns a bar, and I like to eat at the Colorado Mine Company restaurant—but most of the time I prefer just to be up here in the mountains.

I did manage to come down off the mountain, though, to play in the Super Bowl. And the only thing I regretted was that I couldn't take Archibald with me to California. He would have fit in well with all those Hollywood dogs.

"Tom Jackson was the most important player on the team. He was the first player I met when I came to the Broncos, and he acted like we were old friends. He sure made life in the pros easier for me and a lot of other players. Someday we will win the Super Bowl and dedicate it to Tom Jackson."

Keith Bishop,
Broncos guard

20
THE GAME AT THE END OF THE UNIVERSE

EX LIBRIS
PEGASUS

MONDAY, JANUARY 19

Super Bowl XXI, a game so big and so important that it demands Roman numerals. It *must* be the ultimate game. Sponsors are charged $1.2 million for each commercial minute. I'll take three.

I was looking forward to getting to California. I figured we had to be staying in a nicer place than that roach-infested hotel in New Orleans. Newport Beach is classy enough. When we arrived at the hotel, the Newporter Resort, a great place, by the way, there were countless satellite dishes and TV trucks set up, and there were yellow-jacketed security men every few feet. I felt like a rock star going to a concert. This must be the way Michael Jackson feels all the time. There were maybe a couple hundred fans at the hotel. We came in the back way, but they still found us. I guess this is the way it will be all week. We do have a nice view of the harbor in back, the ocean is only a short drive away, and there are no roaches in the room. Floyd Little, the

Broncos' all-time great running back, has a car dealership out here somewhere, and there was a fruit basket in the room from him. Nice touch. I feel bad that Floyd never made it to the playoffs. He quit three years too soon. He was the class of the Broncos for so long.

John Elway wore a pink flowered shirt and baggy pants on the way out here. He said his wife dressed him, and this was his California look. Looks to me like he dressed in the dark. But as long as he keeps leading the team the way he did in Cleveland, I don't care what he wears.

At the airport we sang "Happy Birthday" to Dan Reeves. He's 43 today. He told us the present he wants is six days away.

I just want to get moved in and enjoy the week, regardless of the feeling that we're in prison. We're housed in an enclosed area at the rear of the resort, and they won't let any of our friends come see us in our rooms. So we have to go out and meet them at the gate. You can only touch them through the gate. Is this what Alcatraz was like? I've got to talk to Dan Reeves about changing this policy.

Welcome to California. Where's Disneyland?

TUESDAY

The first meeting with the press. And it was Picture Day. I don't remember it being so crowded in New Orleans. Thousands of media people. Everyone should see this up close once. Only then can you appreciate what the ball players are going through. You can't turn without someone wanting to know what you're doing, what you're thinking, what kind of toilet paper you're using. The press overwhelmed John. Cameras, microphones everywhere. I must have had 40 or 50 guys around me. I guess they want to do the oldest-linebacker story. Everybody's looking for the story nobody else has. The scoop. I've been asked dozens of times already if I'm going to retire.

What I'm really worried about is Friday. This is just Tuesday, and it's a shark-feeding frenzy situation. What happens Friday when all the fans come in from Denver and New York? That's something to consider. It could be a severe mess. I've got to be careful that I don't overextend myself. I did an interview on ESPN tonight and 50 other things today, but the most important thing is to concentrate on the game plan. We've got a feel now for what we want to do against the Giants. I'm glad we're playing them. They're big favorites to win, and when we pull this off, maybe we'll get the notoriety we deserve.

It's good that Dan Reeves has been to the Super Bowl so many times as a coach and a player. He did a good job of preparing us for it. I talked to him today about letting friends and relatives come to our rooms, and he agreed that it was OK. Another slight problem out of the way. We don't need disagreements this week. Our focus must be completely on winning this game.

The point spread is funny. It's 9½, 10 points. They beat us by only 3 at their stadium. I think it goes back to what Chicago did to New England last year in the Bowl, and the bookies saw what the Giants did to New England and Washington, and they just naturally assume that we've got no prayer here. People think those guys are so great that the Broncos can't even stay close.

The funniest thing today was when one reporter came up to me and whispered: "Have you heard that Bill Parcells said the Redskins were the best team they played this year? What do you think about that?"

We had a good practice today. We know we've got to stop Joe Morris. He and I got into it last time when I tackled him and he kicked me. I pointed my finger at him and said, "Do that again, and I'll kick your little ass." He walked away. He's got the real short man's disease. Thinks he's got to prove himself to all the big people. We can't let him break a 50-yarder on us, though. We have to contain him.

I think it's interesting that the Giants have to explain all the time why they're 10 points better than we are. They've got everything to lose. Not only are they supposed to beat us; they're supposed to beat us bad. And if they don't, they're in trouble. We almost beat them without a punter. We never had field position then. It won't be the same. Neutral site. We've got a punter. Natural grass.

I think we have another plus. I expect to see Elway scrambling around from the first play on Super Sunday. He realized in the Cleveland game that he should have been doing that earlier. Dan and some of the others may want him to be a pocket passer, but to be effective he's got to get out and make things happen. I know as a defensive player that, once a quarterback starts to scramble, your defense breaks down. In a zone you're set up to be in a certain spot, and you've got support on both sides. Once a quarterback moves, though, and you begin to move, the zone disappears, and the quarterback has a lot easier time finding an open spot. That's why it works for John. I compare him to Fran Tarkenton. The Minnesota Vikings without Tarkenton were just average. He comes along, and they go to the Super Bowl. They don't win, but they go. Tarkenton could scramble and throw and had those leadership qualities. I see a lot of the same things in John, but I think he's even better than Tarkenton. We sure don't want to lose three Super Bowls.

We had some real fun last night. Went to a place called The Red Onion to eat and have a beer, and about half our guys tagged along. The guy who owns the spot found out we were there and asked John, Ricky Hunley, and me to judge a bikini contest. Ricky has been my roommate all season, but for the Super Bowl, they sprung for single rooms. Thank you, Pat Bowlen.

Ran into some of the Giants. L.T. Mr. Lawrence Taylor. For the first time we really sat down and talked.

Nothing earth-shaking, but I got to know Lawrence better in a relaxed situation. He's a good guy. Bought him 10 cocktails and had them set out right in front of him. But he wouldn't go for it. This is about the only night we can get out and howl, so we stayed out too late. I paid for it today, though. Good thing we didn't practice too hard.

WEDNESDAY

Today was the real "Meet the Press." Have you ever wondered what it was like on my side of the microphone? Well, I took my tape recorder so I could listen later to the machine-gun questions. We sat at tables in the hotel's banquet rooms, like animals in the zoo, and the writers and TV guys paraded by, looking at us.

Q: "Why do you always get the Most Inspirational award?"

T.J.: "Because I get pretty crazy before a game."

Q: "How?"

T.J.: "I start pacing, and I start talking to the other players, trying to fire everybody up. It helps to take the edge off things."

Yawn.

Q: "Lawrence Taylor said he doesn't need to talk to anybody."

T.J.: "He doesn't have to. He makes $850,000 a year."

Q: "But Taylor says he doesn't want to play as long as you have."

T.J.: "I can understand that. Teams key on Lawrence. He may have two or three guys on him. Remember that, as a defensive player, every time you hit somebody, you're being hit, too. It wears you down. I've always been a finesse player. Lawrence is more a power player. It affects your body and wears you down. I've never run through many 260-pound people. I run around them."

Q: "Did you carouse in the last Super Bowl?"

T.J.: "Not me personally. The linebackers went out one night for dinner. I never went to a club. I know that some of our guys, like Glenn Hyde, were out on Bourbon Street partying, and I think when the Cowboys saw that on the news, just like I did, they wondered if we were all doing that. The defense was ready to play, though, if you'll review the game. But we turned the ball over seven times against a Dallas Cowboys offense that had a lot of big-play people, and eventually we couldn't hold them off any longer."

Q: "Are you like Lawrence Taylor?"

T.J.: "In some ways. He's aggressive, and I am. He does a lot with quickness, and that's always been one of my major attributes. There the similarities end. He's so overpowering at his position, and he's got his confidence level up so high. When he first came into the league, people immediately said he was the best linebacker they'd ever seen outside. I think his physical characteristics made him a dominant player. He can dominate a game. If you run away from him, he catches you. If you run at him, he just makes the play. I think our blitzing techniques are similar. I admire Lawrence a great deal. Two years ago I watched a film of their game against Seattle, and I swear in one half he made every play, whether it was a pass downfield or a tackle in the backfield."

Q: "You have an image of being a softer person. He's a hardass."

T.J.: "I think he likes being the bad boy. But I think he's not the mean guy everyone makes him out to be. When he broke Joe Theismann's leg, I don't think anybody felt as bad as he did."

Q: "Are you soft?"

T.J.: "I can get after people if they fire me up. In Cleveland a couple of times I did things I was ashamed of afterward. I gave somebody a late shot after a play, and one of their players asked me what my problem was. I was standing there trying to figure out what my problem was. What problem? My problem was winning the football game."

Q: "But didn't you have a reputation once of being the angry young linebacker?"

T.J.: "Overly so, at times. I got into a lot of fights when I was a young player, but I think that was because people said I was too small, and a lot of bigger guys tried to take advantage of me because of my size. They'd do some things to me they wouldn't try with somebody like Randy White, for instance. I wasn't going to be pushed around. I wouldn't take bunk, and it made me seem angry."

Q: "Is there anything you dislike about being a football player?"

T.J.: "Sometimes the media atten— . . . I'm just kidding, guys. I love you. No, I can honestly say that I enjoy every aspect."

Q: "How do you feel about beating Cleveland?"

T.J.: "Great. They have such ugly uniforms. When I was a kid, I wondered why they didn't have an insignia."

Q: "Does it bother you that their defense has gotten all the attention?"

T.J.: "No, they deserve it. That's a great defense. I've been on a defense that got a lot of attention, in 1977. We were talked about in those terms at the Super Bowl. Maybe somebody should have talked about our 'O.' Maybe they would have played better."

Q: "Are you going to retire?"

Uh. Isn't that where I came in? The same questions, over and over. But that gives you an idea. All they ask me about is Lawrence Taylor and the Giants' defense and a game that happened nine years ago and John Elway. This whole week centers around Elway and the Giants' defense.

John was even interviewed by a Japanese TV network while we were standing there. They had a bit of a communication problem.

TV interviewer: "How your condition?"

Elway: "My ankle? My ankle is fine."

TV interviewer: "Your right leg-ankle, it no hurts?"
Elway: "No hurt no more."
TV interviewer: "How many touchdowns you make?"
Elway: "I wish I knew. Hopefully, four or five."
TV interviewer: "Do you have message for Japanese audience?"
Elway: "Root for the Denver Broncos, the guys in white."

I was hoping we would wear orange, but the Giants were designated as the home team and wanted to wear their blue. The orange didn't help us in New Orleans, but I always feel better playing in the orange. The white uniforms don't seem to have the same power. That sounds stupid, but you always feel better when you look better.

Like Rodney Dangerfield, though, we aren't getting much respect here.

Outside our hotel, there's a gigantic sculpture of a horse, a Bronco, no doubt, made out of old fenders and hubcaps. And we're being treated like something out of a junkyard.

Pat Bowlen finally spoke up today, saying he was tired of the treatment. "The media has been acting like we're some sort of a ragtag operation," our owner said. "It's the same old story. We seem to be the team from out there in the Rockies, just those guys in the funny orange shirts from the mountains. There's been a lot of things in the Los Angeles papers that have mildly bothered me. You know, I think the Broncos are viewed with some disdain by the New York press and the California press and the national press. You get the feeling.

"One story said they ought to let me touch the Super Bowl trophy because that's the only way I'm going to get close to it. I think we're sort of being snubbed a little."

One story, in particular, bothered all of us. It was in

the *Los Angeles Times* and told us not to even bother showing up.

"Dear Denver: Don't bother. Don't go. Don't show. Stay home. Skip the Pasadena trip. Go to Aspen. Do some skiing. Go to Colorado Springs. Climb Pikes Peak. Drop by John Denver's place. Sit around the campfire. Sing some songs.

"Stay away from Super Bowl XXI. You won't like it. The New York Giants are going to be there. They're rough. They're tough. They're good. They're baddddd. They are defensively going to beat you, and they are possibly going to eat you. They are going to bust you Broncos at Alvin Rozelle's Rose Bowl rodeo, so do yourselves a big, big favor. Don't be there."

The thing ended with "Don't go to Pasadena. You can run and you can hide. Crawl under your beds and stay there. The lives you save may be your own."

That kind of talk is pissing us off. We're tired of being treated like someone who doesn't belong here. We earned the right to get to the Super Bowl.

THURSDAY

Everything's beginning to wear me down. It's taken its toll. I think I've handled it, though. I'm keeping myself motivated. It gets to you sometimes, but once I put on the uniform, run the lap, and get a sweat going, I'm turned on again.

I'm looking forward to Saturday, when we get moved to somewhere else and we're alone as a football team. When we move to the other hotel I'm not going to talk to anybody—friends, relatives, press. Well, maybe I'll talk to somebody. It's tough for me to keep my mouth shut for very long. I'm still looking at film every night, keying in on blocking techniques, trying to see if there is something the Giants do that will give it away. A split second can make a difference. When I get out there, I want to react immediately when I see a play develop. I'll know exactly what the Giants are trying to do. I already know all their plays.

I told someone today, and it got big play in *USA Today*, that if this is the ultimate game, then losing is the ultimate loss. I've never gotten over losing in 1978, and if we lose again, I'll never get over it. You don't want to go through life and have people say to you all the time: "Oh, you're that guy who lost two Super Bowls." The Minnesota Vikings have to put up with that all the time, I'm sure. Losing this a second time would be an even more devastating loss. The team will start to gain a reputation for losing.

I couldn't forget the loss to Dallas even if I wanted to. Butch Johnson, who has become a good friend of mine, played on that Cowboys team and made a spectacular catch for a touchdown. Every time I go over to his house I see those seven pictures he has of the catch. He always reminds me.

I'm sensing that we'll be doing a lot of the same things offensively. What Dan has said is that in the past he's tried to put too much that's new into the game plan for a big game. I just hope they'll let John turn it loose, let him scramble and run around and make it happen. But they don't ask me what I think. I guess they're afraid of what I might say.

I don't know what the Giants are doing or thinking, but I'm sure they're confident. But if, at halftime, the score is tied, or we're ahead something like 10–7, they'll be scared out of their pants when they go into the locker room. What happened to the blowout?

If we do get blown out, and I do think about it, then we have to reevaluate how we got here. But I can guarantee that won't happen. I just have a good sense for the way we play. We're going to be in this game, I just know it. Even if the score is 10–0 Giants at halftime, we'll be in it.

My big excitement every night now is to watch the movies on TV, at six bucks a pop. I've seen *Top Gun* twice and *Ruthless People*. And I've ordered a lot of room service. They've got a good burger here. And now I'm getting the onslaught. My friends and my sister Barbara have arrived, and they're pulling me every which way.

I got a telegram from Scott Hamilton, the Olympic gold medal skater. He lives in Denver but comes from Ohio, and we've talked about our backgrounds. He had a lot of problems as a kid but overcame them. Winning the Olympics—that's something. The Super Bowl is close, but the Olympics are only every four years. What if the Super Bowl was every four years?

Today was a hard practice. We banged each other around a lot. Game tempo. At this point my legs are sore, and I'm tired. I had to push myself today to get my work done. But we'll have lighter workouts the next two days. We're beginning to chomp at the bit. We want to play this game right now. We can't wait. The next couple of days will be a distraction. We don't want to lose it before game time. We can't peak on Friday.

FRIDAY

As far as controversy goes, it's been kind of a dull week. I know that bothers the press, but not me. Neither team has been doing a lot of talking. I know I've put a muzzle on my mouth. Vance Johnson has been saying a lot, but nothing that would fire up the Giants. Vance has become our spokesman. He's trying his best to be this year's Jim McMahon.

Our motel is beginning to seem like an apartment house. The wives, the families, the girlfriends have all shown up, and you walk around outside, and there'll be 20 kids playing. It's a strange togetherness, almost as if we all lived on the same block. One big happy family.

I'm glad we've had good security because this would be a heck of a place to make a political statement. I saw the movie *Black Sunday*, where they put a bomb in the Goodyear Blimp and sent it over the Super Bowl. We

don't need anything like that. And I tend to harass
players and fans, so some disturbed person might want
to get even.

I'm still looking forward to doing a number on Joe
Morris since he kicked me in that last game. One more
time, and he's history. I'm just not going to be intimidated on the field.

You know, I keep hearing that sex the night before a
game is not supposed to be good for you. Bull. I
remember Joe Namath talking about what he did the
night before the Jets beat the Colts in that big Super
Bowl upset. A lot of teams, and we used to do this, go
away to a motel the night before a game, even if it's a
home game. When Dan came in as coach, he stopped
that. I guess a lot of coaches think you'll leave your
game in bed. Dan thinks your natural environment is
the best preparation. Casey Stengel, the old baseball
manager, had the perfect attitude. He wanted the players to have their wives and girlfriends with them so they
wouldn't be out chasing women all night and get tired.

My good friend Rick Howard came over last night to
the room, and we drank a bottle of champagne and
watched Farrah Fawcett in the movie *Extremities*.
Well, we didn't really watch. We both fell asleep before
it was over. And before anybody gets the wrong idea,
Rick slept in the chair. Rick has always been my
support. He doesn't live in Denver anymore, but we
were roommates in college and then in Denver for a
while. We made a pact once to be brothers. He's the
brother I never had. And I want him here for my biggest
game.

Nobody's going wild. You've got Keith Bishop sitting
in the lobby, drinking beer with the fans and the press,
and you've got some players changing diapers. I hear
that Pat Bowlen is having a great time. He has a suite
about 100 yards from us, and they've had a couple of
big parties over there. Otherwise, all I know is what I
read in the newspapers. I understand there's a big

Super Bowl party tonight. But not for the players.

This morning I lay there thinking about Morris running weak side. Over and over. When they get inside our 30, they'll depend a lot on that, and I've got to make a difference. I'll have to stuff the lead blocker and try to get him off and make plays on Morris. I've been busting my butt to make sure I can make it happen.

I checked my weight today. Perfect—222. I'll be fast and lean and mean for the game. That's my tradition. My high school coach, Bob Harrison, told me hungry dogs hunt best. Sure, I'll be hungry, but I won't notice until the game's over. Then I'll be starved.

I'm still being asked all the time if this is my last game. I'm trying to keep that out of my mind. In fact, I want to approach this as if it were the first game of my life. After it's over, and I've had time to think—I'm going to Hawaii when the Super Bowl is over—I'll sit on the beach and make a decision.

Had a great evening. Went with my relatives and friends to a restaurant in Laguna Beach and had escargots and lamb chops. My favorite. There wasn't much escargot on my block when I was growing up in Cleveland. In fact, I learned to eat escargots before I knew what it was. When I got out of college, my lawyer took me to an exclusive, fancy restaurant in Louisville. I couldn't even read what was on the menu. He ordered, and I was afraid I'd show how stupid I was. So I just said: "I'll have the same." He had ordered chateaubriand and escargots. I loved the escargots. I asked what it was. Snails. I wanted to throw up. But I still eat them.

Watched the Joan Rivers show because Vance Johnson and Rich Karlis were on it. They didn't seem like football players, except Rich had one shoe on.

My legs are still sore. I'm hoping that will disappear, especially now that we're out of pads.

Practice was very light. We went in sweats. We were only on the field for an hour. Pretty exuberant. I think Dan purposely toned down the practice because yester-

day we almost got four or five guys hurt. Steve Sewell
was on the ground once, rolling around, and we
thought he was badly hurt. Vance took a couple of
heavy licks.

We've got Joe Dudek, the rookie on injured reserve,
supposedly playing the part of Joe Morris in practice.
It's hard to imagine this slow white boy as Joe Morris.
You have to use your imagination. He got cracked once,
and I thought he was dead. I don't mean out. I mean
dead.

Coach thinks we're ahead of schedule.

After practice we came back and had a fish fry with
chicken wings. That's a custom in Denver the Friday
before a game, and we weren't going to screw with
custom. The fish and chicken came in from Denver. No
California wings for us. Two more charters of Broncos
families came in today, and I understand we've got
more than 500 people in our party.

I wanted to go to sleep, but friends kept coming by.
I'm trying to be accommodating. I knew from the
crowd I saw Monday through Thursday that most of
the people would be here today. And things have gotten
madder and louder, especially down in the lobby area.
I'm trying to avoid it.

I did my TV show this afternoon. I really enjoy
television. I've got to believe that I'll end up doing
something on TV. I wouldn't mind being the black John
Madden. Maybe they'd put us together. Wouldn't that
be something? "Hey, fat man, you don't know what
you're talking about."

I had a chance yesterday to go over to the Sheraton to
visit my friend Rick, and I came across a New York
newspaper for the first time this week. I thought it
would be interesting to get their perspective. Those
New York writers are something else. They don't print
what you say; they print what they want you to say.
They take a general statement and change it around.
They're trying to build controversy and make it seem

that we're trying to intimidate the Giants. That's the only time I've been angry this week. If we had another press conference, I'd mention it. But I may not get another chance until after the game. If I were a New York Giant, I'd be saying: "Those Broncos are spouting off at the mouth, and I'm going to find out what they're made of." I guess I've learned something else in case I come back to the Super Bowl in another nine years. Stay away from the New York press.

Today at practice, the defensive backs all changed numbers. Louis Wright was playing safety, and Mike Harden was Steve, and you couldn't tell who was who. A very relaxed atmosphere, but I can sense that the coaches are tightening up. That's the way they are. They can't release their pent-up emotions. I imagine our players will start to tighten up tomorrow when we change hotels and have dinner together. The Last Supper, as it were.

The last part of practice today was Rich Karlis trying to kick a long field goal. We called a time-out on him just as he got ready to kick and made him wait another minute, and then when he did kick it we jumped at him. But he made it. I have a good feeling about Rich's kicking in the game.

Tomorrow we're going to the Beverly Wilshire Hyatt, right there by Beverly Hills and the stars. And the game seems like it's taking forever to get here.

SATURDAY

We moved to the Wilshire Hyatt, and it was a lot quieter, with even heavier security. Mostly what we did today was rest. Ricky Hunley went out with some friends, and one of them turned out to be the brother in the movie *Dr. Detroit.* His name is T.K., and there was another guy with them, someone who produced Janet Jackson's album. They came up to the room. I'm not star-struck, but I was excited about meeting them. They turned out to be good people, football fans, and we ordered up some beers and talked about music, movies, and football. What a combo.

We had a team meeting this morning, much like the one before the New England game, and I was asked by the other players to speak first. I told them that some of us had waited a lot of years to get back to the Super Bowl, and it might be a lot of years before some of them came back, so we really needed to make the most of this opportunity. Don't let it slip through your fingers. What surprised me was that Pat Bowlen got up and gave a real emotional speech about how much the game meant to all of us and how proud he was to be associated with us. I thought he was going to cry. All the players stood up and applauded him when he was finished. We'd like to win for him because he has done a lot for this franchise.

We had our last practice of the year and walked through some things. We went for about 20 minutes, with the majority of the time devoted to a volleyball game. The defensive backs played against the defensive line, and the line won 7–4. Dan even invited the players' wives and families to the workout. You can't say we're not loose. He told us that we had worked hard enough all week to win. "We've accomplished what we set out to do in practice, so we'll have a little bit of fun before tomorrow."

It's now about 4:00 A.M., and I can't sleep. I've been awake most of the night. I'm too keyed up. Wilshire Boulevard is right out the window, and this isn't a soundproof room. I can hear the traffic.

As I lay there earlier I thought about the game one more time. I feel the New York Giants underestimate our ability, and that makes me angry. I figure that has to be a big plus. If they don't blow us out, they'll have to explain to a lot of people what went wrong. I read where Lee Rouson, one of the Giants' running backs who played at Colorado, said they didn't get emotional like us. They didn't have team meetings or any of that stuff.

"We're from the New York area, media capital of the world, with a lot of businesses there. We're very businesslike in approaching everything we do." Well, la-de-da. Sit on it, Lee. I'd like to shove those words down his throat on Sunday.

I used to have a hard time imagining that anyone in China cared whether we won an NFL game. But I understand this game will be shown in China and even Nicaragua and Saudi Arabia and Luxembourg. Do you think they understand the Super Bowl in Luxembourg?

Whatever happens, I'm going to be one of the best-dressed players in the league when this is over. I don't buy that many clothes. It just has never been that important to me. But this guy who makes suits, Rocco something-or-other, came over to the hotel. He took my measurements and said he'd have the suits back to me in a few hours. And he did. Great-looking suits and marvelous tailoring. Just goes to show you: you don't have to wait forever on something when you're playing in the Super Bowl.

I'm going to try to go to sleep one more time and dream about winning the Super Bowl.

"When you're a kicker and miss field goals, suddenly you've got no friends. People treat you like you have a disease. But Tom is my friend no matter what happens. He has always been right by my side when I need him. I just wish he wouldn't call me his paper boy."

Rich Karlis,
Broncos kicker

21
PARADISE LOST;
THUNDERBALL

EX LIBRIS
PEGASUS

Super Sunday started out beautiful. One of those hazy, lazy California days. A long way from Cleveland. A long way from Denver. A long way to go.

The Super Bowl. This is it, sports fans.

Because it was a late-starting game, I had this feeling that everyone was going to get real antsy.

As I've said, I usually don't eat anything on game day, but I started thinking it would probably be midnight before I'd have anything, so I'd better eat a little something. Had some eggs and toast, and I drank a ton of coffee. The team had an informal breakfast down-stairs, but I called room service and kept to myself. The rest of the morning went very slowly. It was almost as if we were in slow motion. I couldn't wait.

Everything on TV had to do with the game. ESPN was replaying every Super Bowl ever played, and I sat and watched that for hours. But when Super Bowl XII came on, I made sure I left the room. On this day I didn't want to be reminded of the disaster of 1978.

The pregame meal finally came around, and I went but didn't eat anything. Mark Jackson was running around looking for the Super Bowl cap I'd given him after the Cleveland game. A bus driver finally found it for him. I grabbed a couple of newspapers and at about 11:45 we got ready to go because we had such a long drive. There was a crowd outside. They had found our secret hideout.

On the bus, I didn't say anything to anyone. I just looked out the window at the California scenery and thought about my career. I was brought into the present and real world, though, when we got to the Rose Bowl. Masses of people everywhere. Some of them were hitting on the side of the bus. I thought I saw a lot more orange in the crowd than blue, which gave me a good feeling. There were three or four blimps in the sky, along with skywriters and airplanes. I hoped none of them would fall out of the sky on the stadium. A few years ago in Baltimore a plane hit the upper deck after the game. Don't get morbid, T.J. I soaked in all the atmosphere. Just me and 100,000 of my closest friends out for a Sunday in the park.

We moved on to the locker room, or what there was of it. This place was almost as small and dingy as Cleveland's locker room. I think the last thing they worry about in a stadium is the locker room. Make the stadium as elaborate as possible and make the leftover space and leftover boards into a locker room.

I started to put my game face on. A locker room is a player's natural environment. Like a deer when he gets back to the woods. There's shelter in the locker room. You can shut out all that's going on outside. The crowd was screaming and celebrating and drinking outside the Rose Bowl, but in that room we were far away from the madding crowd.

Because we had left for the stadium so early, we were in the locker room for what seemed like an eternity. You could hear the music in the distance. The Beach Boys were singing. They had turned this into a real Califor-

nia event. Al Jardine of the Beach Boys was wearing a
jacket that was half Broncos colors, half Giants colors.
Let's go surfing.

Dan Reeves finally came in and announced that it'd
be two minutes until the first group, the kicking team,
went out on the field. Good. Even though I'm a veteran,
I like to play special teams. You can whack people and
make things happen. Time to go out for the first look.
We could burn off some of the energy. I went out and
saw Harry Carson, the guy who pours all that Gatorade
on Bill Parcells. I wished him luck and told him to stay
healthy. He nodded, and I said: "Stay out of the
Gatorade."

The Rose Bowl is incredible. The stands are close, so
you feel like you're in the middle of a bowl. They have
one of those old scoreboards, and everything is painted
green. I love it. This is what football is supposed to be
about, not like those stadiums in St. Louis and Pittsburgh. I did hear complaints about the seating, though.
It doesn't seem like 100,000 people can fit in there at all.
An enthusiastic crowd. You could feel the emotion.
When we went back to the locker room, John seemed
particularly relaxed. He actually yawned while we were
sitting there. Karl Mecklenburg said, "Do you need a
couple of cups of coffee, John, to wake up for this
game?" I just hoped he didn't need sleep.

Dan wasn't emotional in his pregame speech. "Men,
this is what you've been waiting for. You have to play
well in all areas. If you give it 60 minutes and play as
hard as you can, we'll come out of this a winner." It was
pretty much his usual speech. He didn't have to say
much to get us fired up. Any more fired up, and we
would have torn the door down getting out.

Finally, we came out of the locker room, walked
down that short tunnel, and got ready for the introduc-
tions. This may sound melodramatic or something, but
I really was thinking about how far I'd come, how long
I'd been playing, and how well I would have to play. It's
amazing how much you can cram into your mind at

once. For a couple of minutes I didn't even notice all the people. I was alone in the world, alone in the stadium. It started on 121st Street, and it'd probably end here.

I looked at my defensive teammates, especially Louis and Steve. They had been there with me in the other one. Louis looked over, and he smiled. We were thinking the same thing. "Good luck," I said. He didn't hear.

Something did bother me, though. Whenever the defense is introduced, the rest of the team goes on out and waits to meet us. But the league officials had told us before the game that would not be allowed, that the rest of the guys had to stay off to the side while the defense was introduced. The Giants ignored that order. They didn't give a damn. But we played by the rules. What's really funny is that while I was standing there I also thought about the Giants getting 25 tickets each while we got 16. You think about some strange things at a time like that.

Didn't matter. We were going to go out there and kick butt. We were going to show them who the real bad asses are, show them and the 25 people in each of their seats.

I called the toss of the coin, which was exciting because I was supposed to keep the coin as a memento of the game. Talk about irony. The coin, commemorating the Raiders' Super Bowl victory 10 years before, had Al Davis's likeness on one side, John Madden's on the other. And I'm calling it, and I'm getting this coin.

Something happened to the coin, though. The referee never gave it to me. In my haste to get back to the huddle I forgot it. So, Pete Rozelle, if you're listening, I want my souvenir coin.

I called tails. I had been thinking heads all week, but at the moment of the toss, I changed my mind. I don't know why. It was tails, and we got the football. My first good move of the game. One of my few good moves, as it turned out.

The game started, and it began just as I thought it

would. For two weeks all everybody heard about was how great the Giants' defense was and how they were going to contain John Elway and keep him from scrambling against them the way he did other teams. Allie Sherman on ESPN had drawn up the spy technique that the Giants were going to use to keep John from running. So look what he did. On the very first play of the game John ran for a first down. How sweet. Our sideline went crazy. This is what we knew we could do. This is what I foresaw.

John took us right down the field, and Rich nailed the field goal. Three–zip right away. Eat that, Giants.

Time for the defense. We're ready to go. And I get hurt on the first drive of the game. Talk about the worst possible thing that could happen. I didn't realize the significance at that moment. Three times in that drive Mark Bavaro, their tight end, held me. The first time he got away with it. The second time he was called for holding, and they brought the play back. The third time is when I got hurt. It was on a run play the other direction, and Bavaro hooked me. I grabbed him and threw him outside. I came back inside and planted my leg, the right one, and somebody—I don't know who—just rolled into my leg and hit it with his helmet. The knee collapsed. I felt the pain in the interior ligaments. It was the same leg that had been hurt before.

A knee injury. Shit! Not like this. No. But I can't blame anybody. It was one of those fluke things. Bavaro wasn't trying to hurt me. They didn't come after me. A lineman just rolled over on me. That's what's so odd about football. Bob Swenson's career ended on a knee injury, and nobody even touched him. He just made a move back across the field, and the knee tore.

I wanted to stand in the middle of the field and scream. Or cry.

I tried to hide it. I was sure my body would bounce back. The body has an uncanny ability to be hurt and endure pain. Imagine hitting your thumb with a

hammer. There's that initial burst of pain, which is
what I felt when my knee collapsed. But the longer you
wait, the more the pain lessens. I figured that was what
was going to happen here. I didn't want anybody to
know what happened to me.

I was going to shake it off.

At the time I got hurt I was able to keep it from
everyone because we came off the field for a different
coverage.

Steve Antonopulos, our trainer, knew that I was
limping, though. We have a way of communicating. If I
tell him I can play, he goes along with it and doesn't
question me. "Are you all right?" he asked. "Yeah, give
me a few minutes, and I'll be good as new."

I went back in on a short-yardage play, and luckily, the
Giants didn't run my way. On the next play they throw
for the touchdown, and I can try to get myself back
together.

I'm scared. I admit it. This isn't the way I want it to
end.

My leg was starting to hurt, but I knew I had a series
to rest because Ken Woodard and I had decided we
would alternate every series. We wanted to chase a lot
of things down from the backside, and we felt the best
way to do that was stay as fresh as possible. We would
never get tired, and we could put a lot of pressure on
their backside. But what was funny was that they kept
shifting the tight end, so everything was coming in our
direction.

We get the ball back and march right down the field.
It becomes obvious to me the Giants are in serious
trouble. They look so disoriented against John. They
didn't know what he was doing. They were hesitant
about their pass rush—they didn't have a clue as to
whom to cover. One time I saw Lawrence Taylor start to
spy, start to rush, try to get back into coverage, and end
up completely out of the play. I thought it was going to
be a great day because we could score, and that seemed
to be the question mark all week. Could we score much

against this great Giants defense? What we hadn't figured on was that we couldn't keep *them* from scoring.

John got the touchdown on a great quarterback draw, and Ken went in to play defense. We stop them. They punt. We give it back to them, and it's my turn to go back in there.

This is the test. I went in, and the first play was a play-action pass. I had man coverage on Joe Morris. I thought at first it was a run. I took a step forward, and Morris came out of the backfield. I stopped, planted my foot, and tried to retreat toward him. I almost fell down. All I could think about at that point was getting into the line between Simms and Morris. By then, though, Morris had me beat by at least six yards. No way could I get to him. If they throw him the ball, he's got a touchdown.

From what I heard from people watching on TV, it looked like I pulled up like a lame horse. Everyone assumed I had pulled a hamstring or got a cramp. God, I wish it had been a cramp. Nobody realized I was already hurt.

That was it. My body knew it was over, but my brain wouldn't admit it. I didn't want to move. Shoot me right here.

The trainers came out and helped me off. Disaster. I was trying to keep my head up.

The doctor came over and manipulated the leg. He told me to get some ice on it, and they'd take a look at it at halftime. I still felt I could come back at some point.

I couldn't watch for a while. The ice numbed my leg, but when they took it off at halftime the leg started to throb. That leg was killing me. The doctor didn't say anything about giving me a shot or painkillers. All he said was "Tom, it would be very foolish for you to play in the second half. You don't want to be a cripple."

That was the first time I accepted that I wouldn't play again, and I was discouraged. I was back in the treatment room, so before I went back out to the locker

room I put on my happy face. The one thing we didn't
need was the guy who was supposed to be the team's
most inspirational player, the veteran, to be down in the
face or crying when we're still very much in the ball
game. We had played a great half of football. We should
have been up 17–7, but it was 10–9.

We should have been higher than you can believe,
with a lead over this great Giants team. We knew if we
hung in there for a half, they'd start second-guessing
themselves. But that wasn't the case. Rich had missed
two field goals, and we failed to score with a first down
on the one-yard line. Our morale was pretty low. We
should have been blowing these guys out. Instead,
we've let them off the hook, and they're in. If we had
been up 17–7, they would have had to change their
game plan. As it was, they could keep on doing exactly
what they had been doing and wait for it to work.

Just before the half was over—it was a long half
because Super Bowl halftimes always are, not to mention the fact that I'd had the worst news of my life so I
thought time was standing still—the defense started
getting charged up again. One of the players said, "Hey,
they get the ball to open the half. All we've got to do is
stop them, and John will get us another touchdown, and
we'll win this thing."

As we were leaving the locker room, I took off my
shoulder pads and put on a jacket. At that point all the
guys knew it was over for me. They knew how bad I
wanted it, and I think they were afraid to look at me.
When you're hurt, the other players bleed for you. They
knew it could happen to them, too, at any time. My job,
I figured, was to keep everyone's spirits up in the second
half and forget about my trouble.

When we came out, they were playing "New York,
New York." I thought that was a tacky thing to do. Later
on I heard they played "Rocky Mountain High" at the
beginning of the half, but we had that "New York, New
York" ringing in our ears at the kickoff. And Phil

Simms stuck the ball in so fast it made our ears ring even more.

On the Giants' first four possessions, it's touchdown, field goal, touchdown, touchdown. A flood we can't stop. We were just trying to stay out of the way. New York receivers were running wide open. I'm not a coverage specialist, but I know enough to know that a lot of people were *too* open. I saw guys who were so open you couldn't tell who was supposed to be guarding them. When they caught the ball, they were 15 yards away from the nearest defender.

After the touchdown and the field goal, their front seven took charge. They knew John had to throw on every down, and they just cued on him. Now L.T. didn't have to wonder. He knew. They made life miserable for John.

I thought the game would never end. I was so helpless. There was nothing I could do. I felt if I had been out there I could have made a difference. How big a difference? I don't know. Maybe I couldn't have done anything to change the tide, but I will always feel like I could have.

A countdown on a clock in a game that's out of reach usually begins with just about 2 minutes to go. The coundown in the Super Bowl began with about 14 minutes to go. Everyone realized that we couldn't come back, not against that defense, not in this situation. The chances of the Denver Broncos scoring 24 points in 14 minutes were none. The last 14 minutes of my football career I just stood and contemplated a lot of things.

It was time to forget about me and go console some of the other players. The sideline was so quiet. Dan Reeves looked like the blood had been drained out of him. I saw some of the older guys just staring off into space. Nobody could believe it.

CBS made a big deal out of showing me with my arm around John Elway. After the game all the reporters asked me what I told him, but I didn't want to talk about it then. That was personal, between me and John.

What I said was "John, look around at this stadium. You're going to be back here, maybe not at the Rose Bowl. But you'll be in the Super Bowl again, and I want you to remember what losing feels like, how awful you feel right now, how this burns at your gut, to know they kicked our ass, and I want you to think about what winning would feel like right about now. You're a great quarterback. You showed that today again. Don't be discouraged. Come back to the Super Bowl and win it. And think about me when you win it."

John said he loved me, and we embraced. There's a special feeling between him and me, and at that moment, it showed more than ever. We were sharing a heartbreak. We were supposed to be so tough, but we were so vulnerable.

The last thing I said to him was "Thank you. Without you, John, I would have never made it back to the Super Bowl, and you've made the last year of my career a lot of fun. I wish I could be here for the rest of the ride with you. Enjoy it."

Then I went over to Rich Karlis, and he said: "I lost the football game. When I missed those two field goals, I changed the momentum. It's my fault, Tom."

I told him that we wouldn't even have been here if it weren't for him. "You made the kick that got us here, Rich."

Besides, the pressure shouldn't have been on Rich. We should have gone in for the touchdown when we had the ball at the one-yard line. It's that simple.

Mercifully, the game finally ended. I went out and congratulated Lawrence Taylor and told him I still owed him 10 drinks. We laughed for a moment, and then I limped off toward the locker room. Kenny Woodard, the man who will take over for me and carry the torch, was standing there, devastated. We stood outside the locker room and just talked. I told him it was all his. The position he had been waiting for for so long belonged to him. Take the weak side linebacker position and do something good with it, and you'll be back in this game someday soon, I said to him.

The Super Bowl is not only the ultimate victory, but also the ultimate defeat. There's no way you express the emotions, really. You get in the locker room, and everyone looks like he was just told his mother died. Over in the corner is the CBS Super Bowl set, in case we won, and a TV camera that nobody is using. Right about now they're showing the victory celebration in the Giants' locker room. We can hear it in the distance. Nobody wants to get dressed or take a shower. There's no lower feeling. You want to crawl up in a ball and cry. Nobody in life every prepares you for total defeat. I sat there thinking about what was going on in the other locker room. The last thing I saw before I left the field was Bill Parcells being carried off the field, and the photographers surrounding him, and the camera flashes going off in the night air.

It was deathly silent.

Then Dan came in and said, "Make sure you remember what this feels like so that the next time you have an opportunity to play this game you'll want to win so badly you'll never feel this way again. You'll want it extra hard."

We could hear the people chanting outside the windows: "Here we go, Giants, here we go!"

The reporters came in and asked me the questions about my injury and about what kind of difference I would have made on the field. And, of course, they wanted to know if this was my last game.

I answered questions for about an hour, then dropped my head and said, "Look, fellows, I think what I really need to do at this moment is to see the doctor about my leg. I'm sorry."

For one of the few times in my life I couldn't deal with it anymore.

Billy Thompson, who was one of the radio commentators for the game, rode back with me on the bus, and we talked quietly about what might have happened. If, if, if.

What strategy dictated the outcome. We both concluded, and everyone will second-guess about it, that
when you're on the one-yard line, you've got to stick it
in. But all the ifs, ands, and buts would do us no good.
We lost the Super Bowl. We lost it big. Thinking back, I
think the Giants felt that in the fourth quarter they had
to run the score up. Not only did they have to beat us,
but they had to make sure they covered the spread, or
the people in New York who had bet on them would
never accept the victory.

There's no doubt in my mind that the Giants are not
vastly superior to us. They're a good football team, but
we could have beaten them. We should have beaten
them. We let it get away.

Oddly enough, my leg didn't seem to hurt anymore.
Maybe it didn't matter now. I had the rest of my life
for it to get better.

When we got back to the hotel in Newport Beach, I
found it very funny, not laughable, but funny in the odd
sense: all week long there had always been crowds
waiting for us, patting us on the back. But this time,
when the players really needed support, there was
absolutely nobody there. I mean there was no one.

A little later I saw a guy dressed in orange, a "fan,"
who gave me one of the dirtiest looks I've ever seen in
my life. There's no doubt in my mind that he bet the
farm and took the Broncos and the points. I am certain
he was thinking, What an asshole. And I was thinking,
What an asshole. So we were even, I guess.

Victory has a lot of friends, but defeat is lonely.

Someone mentioned on the way back that the loss
cost us a lot of money. We each got $18,000; the Giants
got twice as much. Not once all week had I thought
about that. I wanted the ring. That was worth a lot
more than the $36,000.

I contemplated going to the postgame party Pat
Bowlen was throwing for the team in the hotel, but
once I got back to my room I knew I was in no mood to

join the festivities. I knew the party was planned no matter the outcome, but for me, it was a night for reflecting, not partying.

I ordered some room service, drank some wine, and my good, good friends who care about me came by to give me a hug. I could hear the music coming from the party, and I supposed that most of the players were there. But that was for them.

It's hard to admit this when you're a grown man, but I cried. You dream about being a world champion once in your life, and I knew I wouldn't be. Louis Wright and Steve Foley and Rubin Carter and Paul Howard and Tom Jackson deserved to be, for one day, the best.

I felt like *I* lost that football game. If I had been out there, I would have grabbed our guys by the necks and screamed at them and demanded more from them and made them win.

I'm the guy who goes around and encourages guys like Rich and John and tells all the guys not to get down. This was a time I needed to be embraced, but I had to hide it. That's not the public Tom Jackson.

So I sat in my room and cried like a baby. All I could think about was the frustration of standing there and watching that awful scene. Giants pulling their kids out of the stands and holding them up on their shouldes. Undressing on the sideline and dunking each other with Gatorade.

From now on, before every Super Bowl, when they replay No. I through whatever it is, when they replay No. XII and No. XXI, I'll see the Broncos get blown out and be reminded of what happened. The pain in my knee will go away, but not the pain of those games.

All alone, finally, I tried to put things in perspective. How many guys get two opportunities to go to the Super Bowl and can say they were there nine years apart? Is it better to have loved and lost than never to have been to the Super Bowl?

"I never had to worry about players hustling when Tom was around. He makes practice a pleasure. I told Joe Collier that when Tom is gone the backbone of the Broncos is gone. He means so much to this team, you can't even begin to measure it. The only time I don't like him is when we're in a team meeting and I look at the clock and see that it's time to go, and then I find out Tom set the clock ahead 20 or 30 minutes. He must have done that to me 50 times."

Myrel Moore,
Broncos linebacker coach

22
THE UNDERTAKER'S WIND

Bang the drum softly.

Despite the loss in the Super Bowl, I told the reporters I thought the sun would probably come up Monday morning.

It did.

And Monday turned out to be a little bit brighter than Sunday night. I wasn't recovered but, by Monday morning, I knew there was nothing else we could do but go home. I wrapped the knee tightly, packed my bags with all the souvenirs—the programs, the gifts, the telegrams—swallowed a pill with the last of the wine, and left California behind. We flew back to Denver on a big 747 with all the players, coaches, management, and wives. I couldn't believe we brought so many people to the Super Bowl. We got home late in the afternoon, but there were 100,000 people waiting for us downtown.

I really didn't want to go to a parade, but the city had spent several hundred thousand dollars, and so many people turned out. You couldn't disappoint them.

You've got to hand it to the Denver fans. On Tuesday after the Super Bowl there was a rally for the Giants in the Meadowlands, and fewer than 30,000 people showed up. There are 16 million people living around there, and they didn't care. But our fans did. Somebody was quoted as saying, "What kind of city gives losers a parade?" Yes, we did lose the Super Bowl, but on reflection, we won a lot to get there.

As we rode down the street in open buses, the confetti streamed down, and we waved at the crowd. One of the banners said, "We still love you." And another one offered hope: "Only 184 days until kickoff. Go Broncos!"

We inched our way to the Civic Center through the throng. Just imagine how it would have been if we had won. That's what I regret most. These people deserved a world championship team. They've never had one in pro football or pro basketball, and it's about time.

I thought all my tears had been used up the night before, but they came back when I was introduced. I didn't think people would ever stop clapping. I was asked to say something. "You can't really know how much this means to me. You've welcomed us home in a way we won't soon forget."

Pat Bowlen got up and said, "You took us from the outhouse yesterday to the penthouse today. You really lifted our spirits."

Dan Reeves wasn't prepared for the reception. "I never thought we would have this many people waiting for us when we got back to Denver. This is a special team and a special city, and I promise you we will be back in the Super Bowl."

Dan was second-guessing himself over some calls he made when we had first and goal Sunday. I don't blame him. "That drive eats at you. I've probably come up with 50 plays that would have been better."

Me, too.

The day after, Dan was already talking about what

we needed to do in 1987. He said we needed to get
stronger with our weight program, improve in the
draft, and improve the running game. He also said the
defense would be evaluated from top to bottom in the
off-season months. "I've never seen a team with a
championship when you couldn't run the football and
you couldn't play defense, and both of those things hurt
us in the Super Bowl." Dan said the defense "has got to
be looked at. I don't know that any of us know what the
answers are, but we've go to look at personnel as to
where we can get better. We've got to look at our
philosophy and see where it can be improved, and our
running game is a priority. I think our passing game
can compete with anyone. We've got a great, talented
quarterback, and I think we've improved our football
team at wide receiver. I think our offensive line blocks
for the pass extremely well, but we do not run the ball
well. We were a one-dimensional team, so we've got to
spend the off-season working to change that."

Pat Bowlen was already being quoted as saying that
several players should consider retiring. I think I know
whom he was talking about.

USA Today had a headline on Tuesday morning that
said: "To be No. 1, Broncos don't need a lot." They
quoted me as saying: "Whether you lose by 19 points or
whether you lose by one, I imagine the feeling is the
same. It's a very devastating loss when it happens. But
this is a young team. And there is no doubt in my mind
they will be back, maybe in another time and another
place. A lot of the heart and the dedication that got
them to this game will eventually win this game. Our
young players will have to remember this, and when
they come back, they'll do it right."

I didn't get the MVP award, but John McGrath, a
columnist for *The Denver Post*, gave me the "Worst
Fairy-Tale Scenario" Award—"The sad saga of Tom
Jackson. Instead of making the kind of dynamic contri-
bution that has characterized his career, Jackson, play-

ing what surely was his last game, sustained an early knee injury and spent most of the afternoon on the sideline."

The newspaper had a picture of me as I limped off the plane. The knee still hurt. Despite the wrapping, it hurt like hell on the plane when I couldn't stretch it out. Now, after a long day, it just moaned at me. Dan and I hadn't really talked at length, but he said in the newspaper that he knew "the knee injury had to be bad for him to sit out. Tom wanted to play that game worse than anybody. I've never seen a look on somebody's face like I saw on his before that game."

All for nothing.

The Giants had been invited to the White House.

It was time for me to go off and spend some days in the sun in Hawaii and decide what to do—return or retire.

"T.J. may have been around 14 years, but he's the youngest guy on the team. I hope when I'm as old as he is—he's a grandfather now, I think, and what, about 63 years old—that I have that kind of energy."

Gary Kubiak,
Broncos reserve quarterback

23
BACK TO THE FUTURE

The times, they are a changin'.

Pro football has changed a lot since I came into the game. Back then players were signing for $25,000 a year and happy to get it. Now a quarterback like Vinny Testaverde comes along and wants more than a million dollars a year as a rookie and probably will get it.

The Super Bowl has grown in such magnitude to the point that it's a monster, breeding on itself. I don't know how you'll ever have a game that's as good as all the hype. After all the media and fan attention, anything less than a 43–42 finish, with a team scoring on the last play, is suspect. I don't think there is an answer, though. In baseball, basketball, and hockey you have seven-game series, so the attention is spread out over two weeks and two cities. But in football everything is focused on one game, one city, one mind-blowing event. Maybe they should play a three-game Super Bowl.

The game itself has changed a lot. Instant replays are just one part of that. The most evident difference has

been the change from a running game to a passing
game. When I started, in the Dark Ages, the strongest
teams in the league were those who ran the football the
best. Now, if you can't throw, you can't win. I think our
old defense, the Orange Crush, had a lot to do with the
changes. In 1977, it used to be that you could bump a
receiver until the ball was thrown. We bumped receivers all over the field. John Madden used to accuse us of
raping Dave Casper. I know Casper took a lot of abuse
from our linebackers. We passed him from one linebacker to the next and lived in his jock, and he never did
get in stride. And we checked the Raiders' receivers
coming off the line. You could knock 'em down then if
you wanted to. I remember Casper complaining that we
even tore the back out of his pants. Well, they changed
the rule. One bump in the first five yards. When that
happened, you started seeing small, quick receivers like
Miami's Mark Clayton and Mark Duper, and another
Mark, our Mark Jackson. He's only 5'9" and maybe
weighs 165 pounds. Back in the old days he wouldn't
have lasted a single season being knocked around. But
under the one-bump rule, the little speedy guy can do
the job because he doesn't have to worry about getting
beaten up every game by the defense.

I also, since I came here, offensive linemen have been
allowed to hold. That's all there is to it. Used to be, they
couldn't put their hands out. Now they can grab and
hold, and it's a lot easier to protect the passer. They even
took away the head slap. Defensive linemen would use
that head slap to get around an offensive lineman. Rich
Jackson, no relation, who used to play for the Broncos,
lived off the head slap. Now you can barely touch the
offensive lineman. Everything is set up to help an
offense. I just know it's tougher for a defensive player
than it used to be. Don't even think about hurting the
quarterback.

I think the league feels that what excites the fans is
scoring. That's a business decision. Of course, football

is entertainment. We sometimes forget we're supposed
to be out there entertaining the fans.

We've even gone through a couple of strikes since I
started playing. The first one was in 1974, my second
season, and didn't affect anything, really. But that
strike in the middle of the season in 1982 left an
impression on everyone—players, management, the
fans. Everybody lost in the long run.

Football is a thinking man's game now. Offensive and
defensive game plans used to be a lot simpler. You can
get a hernia carrying the playbook around. We now
have between 150 and 160 defensive combinations. Joe
Collier has one of the most complicated schemes in the
NFL. When I came into the league with Joe, we had
about 30. We actually used only 10 of those. We'd go
out and play in our standard four-three, then later the
three-four, defense the whole game. Now you have
different sets of players for every conceivable situation.
I really think you're better off leaving your best 11 guys
out there, but that's not the way it is anymore. You've
got specialists on top of specialists. I just wanted to play
football. I didn't want to be a designated blitzer on
second down when it was second and seven, or a pass
defender strictly on third down. But that's what the NFL
has come to.

The offenses have dictated a lot of the changes. The
Raiders used to say, "We're going to hand off to Marv
Hubbard and run the ball behind Upshaw and Shell,
and we dare you to stop us. And if you can't, we're going
to run all night." But nobody's like that anymore.
You've got shotgun formations and motions and shifting. Everyone's trying to be sophisticated. What happened to the basics? They got lost somewhere along the
way.

It used to be that you got a feel for the game during
the game, but now that the offenses are more complicated, you can't do that. You study a lot more film, and
the film you look at is broken down in a more sophisti-

cated way. When we were getting ready for the Giants in the Super Bowl, we would look for half an hour at nothing but sweep plays. Then they'd show us a reel of passing plays on third down. Or a whole reel of what they run inside the 20-yard line. We used to just look at game film. Now we might look at three games at the same time.

The players have changed a lot, too. Of course, they thought I was too small to play linebacker. But that was the case in a lot of other situations. Look at Karl Mecklenburg. Before, he would have been nothing but a defensive lineman. But he plays everywhere—linebacker, lineman, both sides, in the middle. We didn't used to have 240-pounders who could run 40 yards in 4.5. Lawrence Taylor would have been a defensive end when I came into the league. It would not have occurred to anyone that a guy that big could also handle a receiver in pass coverage. So you've got smaller receivers and bigger linebackers and more in-betweeners. And the computer doesn't know what to make of it.

One thing players never talk about is that they really do think about losing. "Oh, we don't think about losing," they say. Sure they do. Every big game I've gone into, I've wondered what would happen if we lost. Everybody does. It's natural. But the key is to overcome the fear of losing and not let that be the determining factor.

The most frightening thing about playing pro football is watching your physical skills diminish right before your very eyes. Suddenly, you're a step slower. Suddenly, when you reach to knock down a pass, you're short of the ball. You've always had that split-second reaction time, and it's never failed you. Then it does. In the past, a guy would turn the corner, and I'd close on him. Now he turns the corner, and he begins to pull away. It's a scary experience. I'll give you an example. Here's a reality for me. I've been playing for 14 years, and I've taken a pounding and had a lot of concussions, five or six times when I was left unconscious. I know what it causes. My vision was 20-20 before. Now it's slightly off. I sit in the room with the eye chart, and I can't focus on the seventh line like I could a few years ago.

The league says you can start collecting your pension at 55, but you can get pretty good money if you wait until 65. But you start checking the statistics of guys who hung around this league for 14 years. The average life span is about 59. There's no doubt in my mind that playing pro football has shortened my life. I don't think I'll live to be 75 or 80. My body has been beaten up.

You sacrifice a lot of things in order to play football. But life is like that. Sacrifice.

My body cries at me. I'm sure if I were a CPA, my body wouldn't act this way. Some mornings I can't climb out of bed. My body won't let me. I've got arthritis in some joints, and I have screwed-up knees and a messed-up shoulder.

Every one of those aches has a memory, though.

The worst game I ever played was against the Raiders. We went out to the Coliseum, and my assignment was this rookie named Marcus Allen. He caught two long TDs on me. I was amazed at how awful I was in that game. Later on that pain and disappointment subsided when I found out he was catching long TDs against everyone in the league.

You always remember those snow games. We once played a Monday night game against Green Bay in a blizzard. You couldn't even see across the field. On the very first play I cause a fumble, and Steve Foley picks it up and runs for a touchdown. Then, on the very next Green Bay series, Louis Wright gets a fumble and a touchdown. Who can figure? And wham, we were ahead 14–0. The Pack was way back.

We played a game against New England that started out with sunshine and ended up with a blizzard. The score was something like 38–0 at halftime. I remember hitting Steve Grogan on a blitz and causing him to fumble, and we got a touchdown out of it. By halftime, it was miserable. One of the New England players told me later their coach told them, "Just stay in bounds." They wanted to get it over with as much as we did.

I'll never forget all the games against the Raiders, especially the AFC championship 10 years ago. It could have been yesterday. I can remember almost every play. But you remember playoff games. Maybe if we had been in as many as, say, Dallas, I might forget. But every playoff game was special to me.

You know, I tend to remember the games in Seattle, especially the ones we won, because it's such a tough place to play.

But the coaches indoctrinate you. They keep telling you: "No game is as important as the next one you play." You're brainwashed into believing that.

But you can't forget. There have been so many memorable games. I've played in 201 regular-season and playoff games for the Broncos, and I bet I can tell you about 200 of them. There's one game, though, the last one, I'd like to forget.

During those 14 years there have indeed been a lot of changes in the National Football League. But one thing hasn't changed. It's still a game, and it's still fun to me.

EX LIBRIS
PEGASUS

"To be honest, I was cool about Tom as a line-backer. I'd never seen such a little linebacker. But John Ralston liked him. We thought that was just John, but he was right. The quickness impressed us initially. Then you could see all the other attributes. He's a born leader. He could have been a general in the army. He keeps surprising me. We didn't think he could come back for the '86 season after the knee injury, but he worked harder than he ever has. Nobody has more determination. And Tom had a very good year. He's one of a kind."

Joe Collier,
Broncos assistant head coach

24
CLOCKWORK ORANGE: A PASSION PLAY

I feel very lucky to have played my entire career in one city for one team. That's rare these days. Being stuck in a bad town where they never win—and you know the places I'm talking about—would have been the worst.

Along the way, I've met a few people in Denver, some interesting, others I've already forgotten.

Gerald Phipps and his brother Allan were the owners of the Broncos when I came to Denver. The only way you could really tell them apart was that Allan always wore a string bow tie. Real community-minded. I don't think Gerald ever thought about winning a championship. He just wanted Denver to have a team because that would prove Denver was a big city. I think they always really wanted a major league baseball team, and when they couldn't get it, they settled for football.

Then along came Edgar Kaiser to make money and feed his ego. Kaiser was from the famous Kaiser Steel family, and his money was inherited. So I guess, like a lot of rich kids, he was looking for a toy. He discovered

the Broncos. When Edgar found out all the seats were
sold out in Denver, he just kept raising ticket prices. I
don't think he ever realized how important the Broncos
were to the community. He tried to take the pressure
off himself by making Hein Poulus, his right-hand man,
the bad guy. Edgar tried to make it seem that Hein was
raising prices and causing problems with players' contracts. The best thing ever to happen was that Pat
Bowlen bought the team. Breath of fresh air. He came
in and made a speech to the team about how much he
wanted to win and go to the Super Bowl. Nobody
believed it. At first he seemed like the same kind of guy
as Edgar, a Canadian with a lot of money, and this team
would be just another plaything for him.

But it became evident pretty quickly that Bowlen was
serious. He was around us all the time. His business
became the Denver Broncos. He was young and aggressive. It's funny how I keep getting older and the owners
keep getting younger. I'll tell you what: when we heard
that Bowlen rode a bicycle all the way from Denver to
Greeley, he sure earned our respect. None of the players
could make that 60-mile trip. He was in better shape
than we were. We knew he understood what we were
going through. And he let us know that winning meant
a lot to him. Once we found that out, we started striding
toward the Super Bowl.

I've played for three totally different coaches. I'll
never forget John Ralston looking at us before a game
and saying—keep in mind I do a great John Ralston
impression, but it loses something on paper—"Imagine
that some drunken maniac has just run your car off the
road and killed your wife and child. Think of how
angry you are at him. That's the attitude I want you to
have about your opponent when you go out and play the
game." What kind of nonsense is that? That's sick.

Red Miller was a good, strong, fundamentally sound
coach. Not the best coach in the world, but he did a lot
of good things. He just didn't have much offensive

personnel to work with, and I didn't think he drafted worth a damn, and that put us back for a while. He was a tough man, though. He would get down in the trenches. I remember him showing Claudie Minor a blocking technique, and he got hit and was bleeding and loved it. He walked around with the blood all over his face. He wanted his players to be like that. Blood and guts and not a lot of imagination. Red deserves better. He should be coaching somewhere.

Now, Dan Reeves. I think he's going to be an outstanding coach, one of the best. He's getting the people he wants. He's been through a lot and now understands the potential for failure as well as success. He has grown into the job. When he first got here, we could tell he had molded himself into the image of Tom Landry. He intended to take everything Tom Landry had taught him and use it in Denver. But he found out he had to be his own man, and he finally gained a sense of himself. Dan Reeves talks to his players now. He didn't when he got here. He found out he had to get closer to his players. We're not the Dallas Cowboys. Dan's also learning a lot more about defense. He had never dealt with defense before he got here. So he left it to Joe Collier for a while. He still lets Joe run the defense, but after last season I've heard that he's going to get a lot more involved. That's the way he is. Dan wants something to do with personnel in every area. He's in control of who's going to be on the roster. He makes those decisions. If he feels there should be a change on defense, he makes it. The vote to keep a player could be five to one, and that one vote, if it is Dan's vote, is the only one that counts.

I'm glad to see Joe Collier getting more recognition. He's been my defensive coordinator the whole time I've been in football. Joe's not a screamer, and I think I appreciated that more than anything. He always treated us like men. He didn't jump on our backs. We had a mutual respect. If I had played for someone who shouted at me all the time, I would have been gone years ago.

Joe has such a knowledge of the game. He understands everything about defense. He found out years ago he could get results by just asking instead of kicking butts. He'll ask you to do something impossible, but you'll try because he has asked you. He'll ask me sometimes to defend against a Stanley Morgan in a certain formation for the first 25 yards. The challenge is a thrill, and Joe wouldn't ask if he didn't have faith in you as a player.

I hesitate to call Joe a genius because it's such an overused word in football these days. Everybody who takes a team to the Super Bowl suddenly becomes a genius. But you have to love the fact that Joe has survived five coaches, several general managers, and three owners in Denver. That's a major accomplishment in pro sports. And the defense just goes right on playing, adapting to all the adjustments he's made over the years. He'd put things in for us that nobody else was doing, and five weeks later we'd be looking at film and seeing another team trying our new defense.

People still knock him. Maybe it's because Joe isn't very animated. All the loud coaches, like Buddy Ryan when he was with the Bears, seem to get the attention. Joe's just a gray-haired guy, thin, soft-spoken, wearing wire-rimmed glasses and with a clipboard stuck in his pants. We almost lost him to San Diego a couple of years ago. Don Coryell needed a defensive whiz and offered Joe the moon, I hear. It was killing me. I really believe if Joe had gone to San Diego, Coryell would still have his job and the Chargers would have been a force. But Dan was smart enough to realize he couldn't let Joe go. He gave him a nice raise and named him assistant head coach. I don't think Joe wanted to deal with that San Diego defense, although it would have been his biggest challenge.

Joe has always been flexible. We probably use about

20 different formations in a game, no telling how we'll line up. Our philosophy is that, if the other team wants to attack one guy on our defense, they first have to find out where he is. The thing that Joe does so well is to build his defense around his personnel, not vice versa. If he has great linebackers, then the defense is constructed around them. Now we've got Karl Mecklenburg, and he's the center of Joe's defense. We know we're not going to overpower people that much, so we shift, move and stunt, change our fronts. The element of surprise. And I love surprises.

Myrel Moore is a big surprise. He really is my second father. The Broncos' linebacker coach told the four linebackers years ago, when nobody knew us, that if we worked hard together we could go to the Super Bowl and the Pro Bowl. Well, we went to the Super Bowl, and three of us made the Pro Bowl. And Joe Rizzo deserved to. Myrel and I have been closer than coach and player. When he left us for a while to go to Oakland—what a stupid thing to do—we lost something as linebackers. When he came back—he wised up—that something intangible came back. I'll miss him more than anybody because he turned me loose and let me play the way I knew I could. Myrel wouldn't exactly put his stamp of approval on everything I did, but he'd say on the sideline, "Well, if it's working in this situation, go ahead and continue it. But we don't want to make a habit of it."

The reason the linebackers have been so close is Myrel. We had a drill in which Myrel would stack four tackling dummies in a pile, and the linebackers would be 10 yards apart. The linebackers dive over the dummies and meet head-on. One was supposed to be the ball carrier trying to get over the tackling dummy at the goal line, and the other backer was to try to stop him. When that drill was over, we would be bleeding and tired and frustrated. One time we were sitting in the locker room after that drill, smoke coming out of our eyes, saying, "Can you believe what an asshole Myrel Moore is?" And we looked up, and he was peeking around the corner. We could tell he was really mad. Bob Swenson hollered over at him: "Don't worry. We're talking about another Myrel Moore."

Swenson is something else. I love him. And it's a damn shame his career was cut short. His knee was totally destroyed in a game at Baltimore. I could see him go down behind me. It was like someone blasted him with a shotgun. Watching him was worse than any injury I'd ever had. In the locker room the doctor told me he had torn the knee as bad as it could possibly be torn. I was devastated. I had seen the same thing happen to Joe Rizzo in New England. Three out of four of us went down with knee injuries. One of the reasons I think Randy Gradishar got out when he did was because he had escaped bad injury. He didn't want to be lame the rest of his life. Oh, but we were good there for a while, longer than anyone could imagine about a first-round draft pick, a scrawny fourth-round pick, and two free agents.

The two players who meant the most to me were Randy and B.T., Billy Thompson. Billy passed along his experience and leadership qualities to me, and Randy and I grew up together as pro linebackers and, off the field, grew up as men.

Randy Gradishar. The best. Here was one of the greatest linebackers of all time, and I thought he was going to kill himself sleepwalking. His last two years we roomed together on the road. Can you picture the two of us together? Nobody could. Anyway, in Baltimore we were staying in a motel where the beds were next to each other. Too close, in fact. At about 3:00 A.M., Randy crawled across me, cowered on his knees behind the bed, and screamed, "Tommy, they're in here. They're coming to get us." I woke up scared to death. I thought there were terrorists coming to the room to kill us. But Randy was just having a nightmare. He looked like a baby over in the corner. And this was the guy who was supposed to lead us on defense the next afternoon? I watched him closely on the road after that.

He was naïve, too. One time the Raiders were driving on us and just about to get to the end zone. Randy turned to me and asked me why our fans were booing us. He was sincere. "I think, Randy, it's because of the way we're playing." So Randy goes and stuffs the play on the third down in that patented way of his. Every time a team had third and one against us, they'd run up the middle. Randy would get back seven or eight yards, charge, and meet the runner right at the line of scrimmage, just like Myrel Moore taught us in that drill we hated so much. See, there is a legitimate reason for practice. Over a 10-year period I bet we stopped teams 100 times when Randy did that. He was not bad for a white boy.

I'm awfully proud of John Elway. I've watched him from age 21, and he's a man now. He's a quarterback. Near the end of the 1985 season he threw five interceptions against the Chiefs, but he came back and won the game. Against Cleveland in the AFC championship, with the famous drive, everybody thought John had suddenly arrived. But he had been priming for that moment. He'd been ready. By the time he's finished, he'll be a Hall of Famer and one of the best. I wish I could stay around for it. John Elway will get the Broncos to the Super Bowl several more times. I feel good for him. There have been some great quarterbacks surrounded by real bad teams, and they lost confidence. John just keeps gaining confidence and has handled all the pressure better than anyone can imagine. When it's all over, I really believe John will be among the best quarterbacks who ever played the game.

One guy I'll never forget is our old running back Otis Armstrong. When I was a rookie flying out to camp in Pomona, California, the plane stopped in Chicago, and on stepped a guy in a pink suit. Written in script on his pants is "Otis." He had on a gangster hat. Who is this guy? I thought he was something out of the black Mafia. We get into L.A., and he introduces himself. Otis, my man. He had two lawyers with him. I wondered if that's what I would become.

On the field Otis had great vision. He could see the whole field. He was another guy whose career was cut short by injury. He had a neck injury, the doctors said, but I don't think he ever accepted it. The last I heard, he was suing the Broncos.

Floyd Little was the club's greatest running back. What stood out about him, and I think this is true of all great running backs, was his toughness. Floyd never lost a fight in the locker room. I would have liked to have ended my career like he did. The last game of his career was against Philadelphia, and he made a long zigzagging touchdown run after catching a pass. There are times in your career when you can gear it up for one game, and he did.

A player who never got many accolades and deserved them was Barney Chavous. He was such a great player for so long, but he won't go down in the books that way. He sacrificed a lot for the Broncos. They said he wasn't a good sacker. He always played in a three-man front, and he was supposed to protect against the strongside run. He had to hold his position, while a Lyle Alzado or a Rulon Jones could free-lance and rush the passer from the backside, and I could come on the blitz. So people didn't think Barney was that good. Now when we want to put pressure on the passer, we rush four, five, even six men. If Barney had been young, and we had been rushing six guys, he would have led the league in sacks. But Barney outlived his usefulness, and they came up with some younger players who could play well and made a lot less money. So Barney was told to step aside, even though he had worked harder than he ever had during the off-season and could still play. It happens. Billy Thompson was an All-Pro and could still play in his 13th season, but he was told to retire. They had Dennis Smith, so Billy was expendable. But both Barney and Billy had class. They walked away peacefully rather than blast the team. Sometimes you can't say what you really want because you have to live with these people. But I've never learned to keep my mouth shut.

One of my favorite people was assistant coach Bob Gambold, who went on to Houston. He was coaching the defense for a while, and once we were in a meeting, watching film, when suddenly the light comes on. Bob had fallen asleep, and his chair tipped over and hit the light. How could we get excited if the coach was falling asleep? I've been known to fall asleep a time or two watching films. The hum of the projector after a long, hard night can do that to you. Film study is hypnotic. A guy on another team was telling me about his coach: They sat there in the darkness one day watching film for about 10 minutes, and the coach just kept staring. Finally one of the players got up his nerve and said: "Hey, coach, the film's running backwards." The coach didn't realize it. He was just so caught up in the film. There are coaches like that. I heard that Vince Lombardi would look at the same play hundreds of times. There are some strange people around this game.

Then there was Lyle, and Lyle was Lyle. The only defensive lineman who ever fought Muhammad Ali. They had an exhibition bout during the off-season, and Lyle thought he could make a fortune promoting the fight. Rented Mile High Stadium. Fewer than 20,000 people showed up, and Lyle almost lost his house in the deal. Lyle was wild and crazy. He was impetuous. He did a lot of spur-of-the-moment things that he will probably regret one day. It was the Italian in Lyle. But we worked well together on the weak side. Teams knew we were coming.

One year, though, it ended. Lyle was trying to renegotiate his contract and wanted a no-cut deal. Fred

Gehrke, the GM, said the Broncos didn't give no-cut contracts. So Lyle finds out Craig Morton has one—which he brought with him from the Giants—and Lyle calls Gehrke a liar. In the newspaper. You don't call the general manager a liar and a cheat in the newspaper. You can't take that back. He was traded, of course. After the trade was announced, Lyle called me at training camp and asked if I thought things could be straightened out. I told him it was too late. He was gone. He almost fell off the edge of the earth in Cleveland, but he came back to life in L.A., throwing helmets and playing in the Super Bowl. He fit in perfectly with the Raiders. He and Al Davis were a matched set. They passed a rule in the league called the "Alzado Rule" after he used a helmet to hit some offensive lineman. Now you're not permitted to take off your helmet and use it as a weapon, the rule says. Can you imagine walking up to a tough guy on the street and saying: "Look out, Buster. I've got a helmet in my hands." Now Lyle's the tough guy in all the commercials. Lyle, the movie star.

Rubin Carter should have been an All-Pro. Like Barney, he never got the publicity he deserved. Teams have to push you to the media and to the league. Nobody every spoke up for Rubin, and he was so quiet. He did so much charity work, but because he didn't go around bragging about himself like Lyle did, nobody noticed. All you ever heard was "Rubin is a steady ball player." They made it sound like that was bad.

Louis Wright. Loudini. The magician. Ageless. Competitive spirit. Louis told me that cornerbacks lived on the edge of disaster, and he loved it. That desire to go head to head with a receiver burns inside him. He may be the best athlete on the team. I think I respect him more than anybody on the team.

The new wave of the Denver Broncos' defense is Ricky Hunley. They roomed me with him, I'm sure, to see if some of whatever I had would rub off on him. It worked some. He's still young and doesn't understand everyone's feelings, and sometimes he's only concerned with what's best for Ricky Hunley. He had a lot to learn when he came into the league. He was following a guy whose name will wind up in Canton, Ohio, and it took Ricky a while to figure out that it took more than natural ability. He didn't know much about the history of the linebackers in Denver, and his arrogance rubbed Myrel Moore and some of the others the wrong way. He has a strong ego, but he has spirit, and he's so skilled. In time he could be great.

I've played with more than 200 players in 14 years. Someday I'm going to invite them all over to my house. And maybe I'll invite John Ralston and Hein Poulus and John Madden and Mean Joe Greene, too. That would be some party.

"Don't pay any attention to what T.J. says about retirement. Tom Jackson will never quit the game. The only way they'll ever get him out of football is to take him behind the blocking sled, tear his uniform off, and shoot him."

Steve Foley,
Broncos free safety

25
WHAT AM I GOING TO BE WHEN I GROW UP?

EX LIBRIS
PEGASUS

It's so peaceful in Hana. I can disappear into the waves or woods.

The isolated east side of Maui in Hawaii was a good place to get away from the disappointments of the Super Bowl.

Hana is at the end of a dangerous, snaking road. The only way to beat that road is to blitz it.

I did, at night, in the rain. Two cars can barely pass on that narrow, winding stretch of highway, and I was stupidly whipping around the curves, trying to get over what had happened in California. Then I saw a sign that said: "Road Narrows." Slow down, T.J. It's not time to die.

There are these cliffs in Hana, and if you ever want to go and sit and think and not be bothered, the perfect spot is behind cabins 7–11 in Waianapanapa State Park. I needed to make the most important decision of my life. Should I retire? Should I continue playing? Should I continue playing someplace else? I sat up on those cliffs for a couple of hours and thought about it.

This is the kind of decision nobody else can really help you with. My own Lady Di can offer advice. Friends can give you their opinions. And, of course, the team—Dan Reeves and Pat Bowlen—will tell you what they're thinking. But, in the end, it's something you must decide for yourself.

The first choice was easy. I'm not going to another team to finish out my career. Denver is my home; the Broncos are my team. I'd never feel right playing for anyone else. So I scratched that.

So many people told me to keep on playing. I could get over it. Everybody I met said: "Please don't retire, Tom. You're playing so well." People I didn't even know. People in Hawaii. Of course, their opinion was prejudiced by my presence. But it makes you think.

I still felt good. The doctors told me the knee didn't require surgery. It needed rest and another off-season of rehabilitation. I've got the routine down now. I soaked it in a lot of salt water in Hawaii. Even though I already have a pretty good tan, I spent a lot of time on the beach, soaking the knee.

If I came back, I'd just have to work hard again in the off-season. But I honestly felt 1986 was one of my best seasons in several years. I don't feel 35. There are some scars, and there are some aches. But I'm holding together. Physically, I don't feel like retiring, I told myself up on the mountain.

Reeves had been serious when he said overhauling the defense would be a priority. There had been talk on the streets that a rift had developed between Joe Collier and Dan. I never saw it, and I don't believe it. I think we were all frustrated at what happened at the Super Bowl. Dan got up at the Colorado Sports Hall of Fame banquet and told everybody there were no problems between him and Joe. "I've got the best coaching staff in football," he said.

The coaches were talking about trying to beef up on

defense. There was a kid on injured reserve who they thought would make a good outside linebacker, and they were looking at some other defensive monsters. It was being said that teams finally realized they could beat our defense, which relied on quickness and finesse, by coming right at us, just banging on us. So there was talk that we would be making some severe changes in 1987. Bigger people, more man-to-man pass coverage, and, ah!, more blitzing. Sounded like fun.

But, on the other side, I'd had some conversations with people from the networks. NBC was interested, and ABC had talked to me about doing some things. Maybe this was the time, if the timing was right. I don't have to make a lot of hasty decisions in order to make money. I've saved my money, and I'd had over a million dollars deferred by the Broncos. So I was in good financial shape. Nobody has to feel sorry for Tom Jackson. I feel sorry for all the guys who didn't protect their money or turned it over to the wrong people. I was reading that Kareem Abdul-Jabbar had lost millions to his agent. Maybe that's why he kept on playing. Joe Louis died broke. I saw a piece on TV about a guy who used to play pro basketball, John Williamson. He was making big money at one time. Now he's a night watchman and is back living in the projects where he grew up.

Fifteen years would be a good round number. Just one more year. Maybe there would even be another Super Bowl next season. But do you hang around too long? Do you stay past your welcome? Would the Broncos cut me in training camp? The same fear I had as a rookie resurfaced. Would they do to me what they did to Barney Chavous? Or would they really want me around? Would I get hurt seriously? Would I be terrible? Would I be an All-Pro again? Would I intercept the big pass? Would I drop the ball?

It's not easy being orange.

What do I do?

For a while I watched the ocean and cleared my mind. Then I walked down the cliffs and worked up a big smile.

T.J. was retiring.

It was not the easiest thing to walk away from the Broncos and away from football, though. I did have second thoughts, I admit. People came up to me all the time after I came back from Hawaii and said, "You have to come back for another year. You can't quit now." I could tell, however, that the Broncos were equally as ready for me to retire; hints were coming out in the newspapers. But I wanted to sit down and talk with Dan Reeves before anything was official, and I wanted to do it before the draft. Besides, I was getting tired of everyone saying, "What you going to do about retiring, Tom?" It seems like everyone I met on the street asked the same question over and over.

On the first of May, Dan and I looked at each other across his desk, and we both knew. "Dan, this is it for me." He didn't try to talk me out of it. He said he'd like to keep me around the club, use me as a coach in training camp or something. But I didn't know. Was it time to make a clean break? We decided we would hold a press conference the next day and announce my decision.

I came to the office early that day, snuck in the back door, and went up to Myrel Moore's office. We talked for a while, and I tried to laugh it off. I was actually in good spirits. At five minutes to one, Dan came in and said: "Let's go do it, T.J."

When I went into the conference room, I was taken aback. There must have been a hundred or more people from the press waiting. I thought maybe there would be a dozen or so. Suddenly it hit me. Maybe this is bigger than I had imagined. I remembered when Billy Thompson retired and how sad everyone seemed. I didn't want it to be like that.

But I started talking, and I saw Myrel Moore in the back crying. It was all I could do to hold on. At that moment, I thought about my dad. I had called him the night before and told him I was through, and he seemed happy. He always wanted me to leave the game walking, and I would. My body is sore and has some scars, but I won't limp through the rest of my life, and won't be confined to a bed or a chair. I think that's what my father wanted more than anything.

The first thing I said, to break the ice, was: "Does anybody know where I can get a job making $300,000 a year?"

Everyone relaxed a little. But it was still tough. I don't remember a whole lot of what I said, except that I did want to be remembered alongside old No. 79, Barney Chavous, who was also retiring. All the old gang was just about gone. Rubin Carter would be retiring a few days after me. The linebackers were all gone—Randy Gradishar, Bob Swenson, Joe Rizzo. In fact, the only teammates left from the 1977 Super Bowl were Louis Wright, Steve Foley, and Paul Howard, and Paul probably wouldn't play again. It was time to move over and let Woodman—Ken Woodard—take over at linebacker.

I closed the press conference this way: "I guess I played pretty good weakside linebacker here."

I guess so.

After the press conference Myrel, Randy, Woodard, and I went drinking and talking football at the bar at the Holiday Inn. I had a little too much to drink and finally wandered home. When I woke up the next morning and saw the headlines in the newspapers I knew it was official. I was no longer a pro football player.

I got up and went out for breakfast and couldn't wait to see someone I knew. For so long everyone wanted to know if I was going to retire. Now they all knew and wouldn't ask me that question any more. I went into the restaurant, waved at someone, and heard: "So what are you going to do now, T.J.?"

A new question.

Everybody wants to know what I'm going to do now.

Well, I flew to New York and auditioned for NBC, and we agreed to a deal that day, so I'll be doing some commentary on the AFC games, and I'm excited about that. I think my future is in the media. I have such a pretty face. And the one thing I know is that I'm going to be myself. Dizzy Dean was himself. John Madden is himself. And T.J. is going to be T.J.

So, the day after the press conference I took my basketball and went to my old apartment complex and just played ball for a while. No pressure. No questions. No problems.

Good-bye, pro football. It's been real.

I will remember the NFL. I hope it remembers me. I would like to be remembered as a consistent player, one who always tried hard, a player who cared about the game.

Now, I'm going off to challenge the world.

Does anybody need someone who can blitz?

So what do you want to be when you grow up, Tom Jackson?

I never want to grow up.

"At training camp one night years ago Tommy Jackson asked me to go with him to his car. I assumed he had a major-boffo, exclusive, secret, deep-background scoop for me. Instead, he wanted me to listen to his new Luther Vandross tape on the new stereo system in his car. We sat there in the heart of darkness singing as loud as we could. Tom and I had come to Denver about the same time, and our successes had paralleled. He had developed into an All-Pro, the club's most inspirational player, and a community leader. I had gotten a $25-a-week raise. Tom was one of my all-time favorite players, just behind Bob Cousy. Rarely do you find such a quality person. 'You've got a story to tell. Maybe we should write a book,' I said to Tom that night. 'Maybe we will someday,' Tom said."

Woody Paige

26
FINALLY

I was the last one to leave the locker room after we beat New England in the playoffs. My last home game. Maybe I should have turned out the lights. "Turn out the lights; the party's over."

I just didn't want to let go.

Fourteen seasons of coming into this locker room, in bad times and good. My little orange-and-blue cubicle was a second home for me. More than 100 times for regular-season games. Another 30 times for exhibition games. And four home playoff games. The defensive players over on this side, the offensive players on the side nearest the field, with John Elway's locker right next to the door. You don't want your quarterback to walk farther than he has to. I went over and congratulated John. Dan Reeves and I shook hands, and Myrel Moore walked by and put his arm around me.

I also had been the first player in the locker room after the game ended. I didn't stay around to shake hands with the Patriots. As I ran off the field I saw John

Denver, the singer. This was a good time to be singing "Rocky Mountain High." You couldn't be higher than this. I waved up at the fans in the south stands, ran in the door, and settled down in front of my locker to rest for a moment.

So many people wanted to talk afterward about the team playing in Cleveland.

"How does it feel, winning this game and going back to Cleveland?" the radio guy asked.

"It feels like I've come a long way in a short time."

I didn't think I'd ever get the uniform off. But at last the crowd broke, and I grabbed a shower and returned to find another group of reporters. All four television stations wanted an interview, and I was being pulled in every direction.

Finally I had a few minutes to myself. I looked around the room. Everybody was gone. The room was empty, and it was quiet. Time to go.

I walked outside into the darkness.

A bunch of youngsters were waiting outside for the last autograph.

"OK, guys, I'll sign every one, but let's start walking toward my car. It's been a long day and I'm tired." Someday they may not want my autograph. Besides, my philosophy has always been that, if they care enough to ask, I should care enough to sign.

When we got to the car—a Ford Bronco, what did you expect me to drive?—I finished signing the scraps of paper, a program, a pennant.

The cool night air felt good. Winning felt good.

Across the way in the parking lot several kids were playing a pickup game of touch football. I stood and watched.

What the hell?

I walked over and said, "Hey, could you guys use another player?"

I love the game, whether it's on 121st Street, in the

Rose Bowl, in the Superdome, in the Los Angeles Coliseum, on the practice field in Greeley, in Mile High Stadium, or on an asphalt parking lot in the dark.

Suddenly I was no longer tired. It was five on five, and the other side had the ball. They snapped it.

And I blitzed.